# SMALL TOWN INTERNET MARKETING

How to Use the Internet to
Promote Your Local Business

© 2017 Jerry Work

All rights reserved.

Reproduction or translation of any part of this work beyond that permitted by Section 107 or 108 of the 1976 United States Copyright Act without permission of the copyright owner is unlawful. Requests for permission or further information should be addressed in writing to Jerry Work.

This publication is designed to provide accurate and authoritative information in regard to the subject matter covered. It is sold with the understanding that the publisher is not engaged in rendering legal, accounting or other professional advice.

To learn more about the services offered by the author, visit www.WorkMedia.net or email Info@WorkMedia.net.

# Table of Contents

**Introduction** .................................................................................. 9

**Understanding Internet Marketing** ........................................... 11
- What Is Internet Marketing? ..................................................... 11
- The Components of an Internet Marketing Campaign ............ 12
- Marketing Budgets .................................................................... 15

**Your Website** ............................................................................... 17
- WordPress ................................................................................. 19
- Design Considerations ............................................................. 20
- Copy .......................................................................................... 23
  - Content Updating ................................................................. 25
- WordPress Configuration ......................................................... 26
  - Permalinks ............................................................................ 26

**Search Engine Optimization** ...................................................... 29
- Keywords ................................................................................... 29
  - How to Do Keyword Research ............................................. 29
- On-page Optimization .............................................................. 33
  - Page URLs ............................................................................. 33
  - Page Titles ............................................................................ 34
  - Copy ..................................................................................... 34
  - Meta Tags ............................................................................. 35
  - Cross-linking ........................................................................ 36
- Site Maps .................................................................................. 39
  - HTML .................................................................................... 39
  - XML ....................................................................................... 39
- Links .......................................................................................... 40
  - Trust flow .............................................................................. 41
- Your Domain Name .................................................................. 42
- Google Webmaster ................................................................... 43
- Website Load Speed ................................................................. 46
- Mobile Friendliness .................................................................. 48
  - AMP ...................................................................................... 48
- Ranking Tracking ...................................................................... 49

**Local SEO** .................................................................................... 51
- Local Optimization ................................................................... 51

Google Business .................................................................... 52
Citations ................................................................................ 54
Local Directories ................................................................ 54
   Yelp ........................................................................................ 55
Reviews ................................................................................. 57
   Instructions for Leaving Social Media Reviews ................. 57
Local Offers ......................................................................... 59

## Paid Search ................................................................................ 61
Cost per Cilck ....................................................................... 62
Cost per Conversion ........................................................... 62
Google AdWords .................................................................. 63
   Campaigns and Ad Groups ................................................. 63
   Conversion Tracking ........................................................... 65
   Geographic Targeting ......................................................... 67
   Keywords ............................................................................... 67
   Dayparting ............................................................................. 70
   AdSense (Content Network) Ads ...................................... 70
   Dimensions ........................................................................... 72
   Ad Extensions ...................................................................... 72
   Remarketing ......................................................................... 74
   Negative keywords .............................................................. 75
Bing Ads ................................................................................. 75
Split Testing ......................................................................... 76
Paid Search Landing Pages ............................................... 77

## Social Media ............................................................................. 81
Google+ ................................................................................. 86
Facebook ............................................................................... 87
Memes .................................................................................... 91
Going viral ............................................................................ 92
Facebook Advertising ........................................................ 93
YouTube and Videos ........................................................... 98

## Email ............................................................................................ 99
Email Marketing Companies ............................................ 100
Email Signup Form ............................................................ 100

## Analytics .................................................................................. 101
Conversion Tracking .......................................................... 10

**Other Internet Marketing Strategies** ........................................ 107
    Increasing Search Shelf Space ........................................ 107
    Craig's List ........................................................................ 108
    Expired Domain Names .................................................. 109
    Content Aggregation ....................................................... 110

**Conclusion** ............................................................................. 113

# Introduction

My name is Jerry Work. I live and work in Dickson, Tennessee, about a half-hour drive West of Nashville. I am a professional Internet marketer and have run my own company, Work Media, for over a decade.

I have had the good fortune to work with some of the biggest companies in the world. I have worked with law firms. I have worked with the makers of the finest barbecue sauce in Memphis.

And I have worked with small town local businesses.

And boy do they need some help.

Hey, I'm glad about it. If it were too easy, I would be out of business. You're busy running your business. You're overworked and stressed out. Who has time to study Internet marketing?

It is really not that hard to conduct an effective Internet marketing campaign. You just need a system. And you need some time. I can't give you the time. But I can give you the system.

Now, if you read all this and decide that it's just too much work - call me. Or call somebody. Don't just walk away from the idea of using the Internet to promote your business. It's too important.

That's why I made the decision to write this book. You shouldn't need an MBA to understand this stuff. So I've tried to give you a pretty good overall view of the different parts of an Internet marketing campaign, with just enough detail so you can dig in and get your hands dirty.

Let's get to work.

# Understanding Internet Marketing

## What Is Internet Marketing?

Internet marketing is using the Internet to promote your business, which could mean Google, Facebook, an email list, mobile phone advertising, or any number of similar technologies.

Promoting your business online has a few advantages over traditional media marketing, like radio and print ads. These include:

- Online ads can be changed instantly. It can take days or weeks to change a traditional print, radio or TV ad.

- Ads can be automatically split-tested. Running two ads at once and comparing results can help you improve your ad performance.

- Budget can be changed any time. Need to run an ad for one day but only have $5? No problem. You can be on Google this afternoon.

- A growing advertising market. Everybody has a smart phone now. Everybody is using his or her phone to search for information. Businesses that take advantage of that will gain a competitive advantage.

- Personal connection. Internet marketing, and social media in particular, creates a communication channel that is much more personal than any kind of traditional media.

- Targeted marketing. Internet marketing can put your business in front of people looking for the exact thing you are selling.

There is a lot to like about Internet marketing.

## The Components of an Internet Marketing Campaign

There are five main components to Internet marketing as I see it:

- Your website
- Search engine optimization (SEO)
- Paid search
- Social media
- Email

A sound Internet marketing strategy makes use of all five of these components to some degree. The picture below illustrates how these components work together.

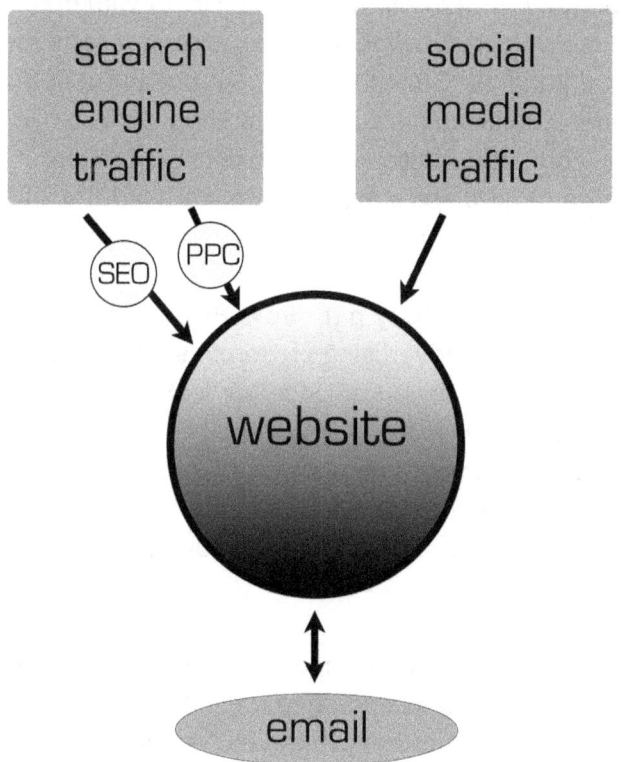

**Your website.** Your website is like your own little piece of Internet real estate. So step one is to build a website for your business. You don't want to depend on any kind of third party platform like Facebook to represent your business. Facebook could change all their rules or go out of business next week, and then you wouldn't have any real estate. With your own website, you're in control.

**Search engine optimization (SEO).** This is the process of optimizing a website so that it appears highly in organic (non-paid) search engine results for specific target keywords. So if you own a computer networking business in Dickson, Tennessee, you would want your website to appear prominently in Google when someone searches for "Dickson TN computer networking." The things you do to make this happen are called SEO.

There is a category of SEO that deals specifically with optimizing a local business website to appear in local search results for its geographic market area. So in this case, our computer networking business owner would like his business to show up for anyone searching for "computer networking" who is in the Dickson, Tennessee area, regardless if they include the word "Dickson" in the search or not.

**Paid search, also called "pay per click (PPC)".** This is using one of numerous online advertising platforms such as Google AdWords or Bing Ads to drive traffic to your website. It generates the same result as SEO, with the difference being that you actually pay a certain amount of money for each click. Included in this general category is the process of running graphical ads on third party (non-search) websites using an advertising platform like Google AdWords.

**Social media.** Facebook, Twitter and Google+ can all generate awareness for your business and drive traffic to your website. They also provide the opportunity to have one-on-one conversations with prospective customers. If you're going to use these to promote your business, you've got to be more strategic than just doing personal Facebook updates.

**Email.** I will make the wild assumption that you know what email is. In terms of Internet marketing, what we are talking about is building a list of email addresses of prospective customers to whom you send some kind of regular communication like a newsletter.

When it comes to marketing and promoting your business on the Internet, you need to think 'multi-pronged." In other words, don't just use one strategy. Use a combination of different strategies to get your message out.

The great thing about Internet marketing is that many strategies don't require money. Only time. Now, time is the most valuable thing there is - but if you don't have money, then time is what you have to spend. And if you don't have enough of your own time, maybe you can spend somebody else's time. Got a teenage daughter who is in AP English? Perfect. Put her to work writing blog posts for your website or updating your Facebook page.

Every Internet marketing strategy discussed in this book can be pulled off yourself with a combination of your own ingenuity and whatever kinds of deals you can work out with people who can help you with the parts that you can't do.

Of course, you can always hire an expert. In that case, the information in this book will help you have a good understanding of the kind of help you need.

We'll start with a discussion of your website because that comes before all the other components. Then we will proceed to search engine optimization, which is the process that should start as soon as you have a website. Then we'll work our way through the other strategies.

But first, a little bit of marketing math...

## Marketing Budgets

When you think in terms of "budget', you are generally assigning a fixed dollar amount to spend over a fixed amount of time - i.e., $1,000 per month.

A better way to think about marketing is in terms of cost per acquisition, or return on investment, as explained below.

**Cost per Acquisition**

This is how much it costs you to get a customer. If you spend $1,000 on marketing and get 5 customers, then your cost per acquisition is $200 ($1,000 divided by 5). Sometimes this is hard to figure out with a whole lot of certainty. But it's easier in the Internet world than the real world.

**Return on Investment**

This is how much you generate in revenue above the cost of advertising. So if for that $1,000 you spent above, you made $5,000, then your return on investment is 4x, or 400%, because you made $4 in earnings for $1 you spent ($5 revenue minus $1 spent on advertising).

In a later chapter, we are going to talk about conversions and conversion tracking, which are how you can make the above types of calculations.

# Your Website

So the first question is:

Do you have a website?

If the answer is yes, the next question is:

How old is it?

If your website is more than a few years old, it is probably time for a new one.

Internet marketing technology changes constantly. Google has recently begun placing a LOT more emphasis on mobile friendliness and load speed in ranking websites. Older websites usually don't pass the test.

If you do not yet have a website, then that is step one.

To have a website, you need two things: website hosting and a domain name.

**Domain Names**

Your domain name is your friendly website address. It usually will relate to the name of your business or what your business sells. So it could be www.JacobsJones.com, or something like www.Dickson-Real-Estate-Law.com.

You never really own your domain name. It must be renewed (and paid for) periodically, although you can renew it for more than one year at a time. At a minimum, it must be renewed annually. The cost will generally be around $15 or $20 per year for a .com domain, although other non-.com domains may cost more or less. Although there are all kinds of different domains you can register these days, I would still go with a .com if you can find one that works for you. My second choice would be a .net.

**Website Hosting**

There are places on the Internet that let you set up a website for free, such as WordPress.com. These types of sites do not require their own domain. But if you are serious about promoting your business online, then you're going to want to have your own domain name. That means you're going to have to have hosting.

Hosting is simply some space on a server (a certain type of computer connected to the Internet) where your website files can reside. The server "serves" your webpages to a person when he or she types in your web address in a program called a "browser."

You don't have to worry about the technical details. You just need to find a company you like and sign up. Companies that sell domain names are called "registrars." These days, most registrars also offer hosting. It might be easier to purchase your domain and hosting from the same company. The biggest and most well known domain registrar/hosting company is GoDaddy. But there are lots of other options.

If you are a local level business, then you will probably be just fine with a low cost shared hosting account. Shared hosting means there are multiple websites (sometimes hundreds) on the same server. The advantage of shared hosting is that it is cheap. The disadvantage is that, with so many websites crammed onto the same server, shared hosted websites tend to be slower and less reliable.

A step up from standard shared hosting is something like a managed WordPress account. This is a type of shared hosting plan that is optimized for WordPress (which we will discuss later) and may be on a server with fewer other sites. It might cost a little more. Two options for managed WordPress hosting are GoDaddy and WPEngine.

A big step up from that is a cloud hosting account. With cloud hosting, the website files are spread out among hundreds of different servers. It tends to be a lot more expensive. This is what I use for my business and the client sites I host. It is robust and very reliable.

Finally, you can even have your own dedicated server. This is by far the most expensive and complicated option. Unless you expect your website to have many thousands of visits every day, that is probably overkill. Not recommended.

Once you have a domain name and hosting, you have to create the pages that comprise your website. In their simplest form, Web pages consist of nothing more than text files coded with a sort-of scripting language called HTML ("HyperText Markup Language"). It would be possible for you to create your entire website using nothing more than a simple text editor. But these days, most websites are far more sophisticated than that, consisting of many different types of files that work together.

A better approach than doing everything manually is to build your website on a platform that creates all these files for you, so that all you have to do is log in and add your content. The most popular platform in the world for accomplishing this is called WordPress.

## WordPress

If you are comfortable with technology, then you can certainly install WordPress yourself on a hosting account and begin using it. Or you can purchase pre-configured WordPress website hosting through a company like GoDaddy or WPEngine. Easiest of all is to pay an experienced website developer to do it for you.

A default WordPress installation is not all that attractive, but you make it more attractive and modern looking by installing what is called a "theme." A theme is a collection of files, templates and stylesheets that give the website a particular look. Taking it a step further, you can install any number of thousands of plugins that extend the functionality of WordPress and give you lots more flexibility with what you can do with it.

If you go with WordPress, there are companies now offering hosting just for that, and that might be a good idea to get the best performance. Here are the companies on the official list of WordPress hosts:

- Bluehost
- HostGator
- DreamHost
- InMotion Hosting
- SiteGround

If you are going to be hosting multiple websites, or in a situation where you could have heavy traffic, then you might want to invest in something like cloud hosting.

In your domain registrar account, you configure the domain so that requests for your website point to the right server. If you use separate domain and hosting companies, you will have to configure this manually. If you use the same company for both, it will probably be done automatically.

## Design Considerations

You don't have to have the most beautiful website in the world. You don't have to look like a Fortune 500 company. But there are a few rules you should follow to have better success using your website to promote your business.

To start with, your website should look like what websites look like today. Have you ever looked at a website that was built 20 years ago? It will look very dated. The images may not be crisp. It may not even be readable at all on a mobile device. This is not what you want. You want a site that is clean, easy to load, easy to navigate, and that is very functional on a mobile device.

Website load time is VERY important. Search engines hate slow loading websites. So do people. Large images and a number of other things increase the amount of time it takes for a web page to load.

Here are some other rules for your website on mobile devices:

- Use large, easily readable fonts.

- No scrolling to the side.

- Easy navigation (often in the form of a dropdown rather than buttons).

There are two ways to deal with mobile. Your website can either send different web pages to mobile devices, or the website can use stylesheets to reformat itself for mobile (called "responsive" design). The responsive option is the best way to do it, and what Google prefers.

Here are a couple of examples to highlight what I am talking about as far as good design versus bad design.

## Good Mobile Design

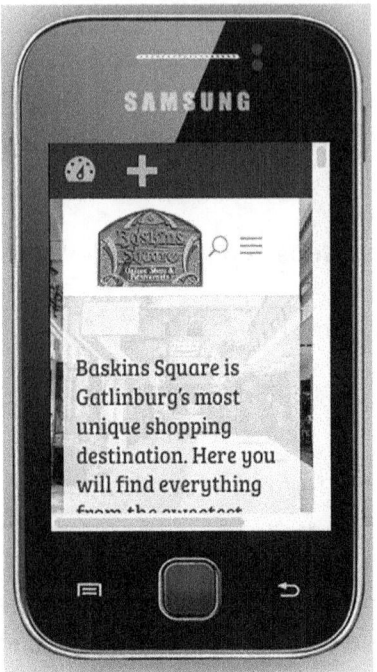

Notice that this website is very usable on this small phone screen. The logo fits into the top of the screen with a dropdown menu next to it for easy navigation. The text on the screen is nice and big and easy to read. There is no side-to-side scrolling.

**Bad Mobile Design**

Sorry Dickson County government, but your website looks crappy on this small screen. You can only see a tiny portion of the page and are going to have to scroll to the side several times to read all the way across. To see the different menu options, you will have to scroll sideways as well.

I could fill up a whole book about WordPress or website design in general, but that is not really our main point. If you need help setting up a website, find a qualified developer and your life will be a lot easier.

## Copy

Let's talk about the words on your website. Here are some rules to follow:

- Try to have at least 300 words in the copy on the main pages of your site. The more, the better.

- Use short sentences.

- Use shorter words whenever possible.

- Break your copy into short paragraphs.

The more words on your website, the better. But also keep in mind that reading on a screen is stressful on the eyes. Using short words, sentences and paragraphs makes reading easier.

Add new content to your website on a regular basis. There are a few good reasons to do this. For one thing, search engines like it. Google tends to favor websites that update often. The most typical way to update your website is through a blog. Your blog is the part of your website where you can post articles or commentary about your industry, your town, or whatever.

Adding new content gives you a way to get your website ranked for more search terms. Every new page or blog post should be written with a particular keyword in mind. More about that later.

Blogs, articles and the like allow you to showcase your knowledge about your industry. Even if you are a small business performing a service at a local level, it allows you to demonstrate your expertise. It also creates content that you can filter through your social media accounts.

Let's say you're an accountant in a small town called White Bluff. Every time you update your website with some kind of blog post or article, it encourages Google to display your website in search results. And it gives you material to use in updates on your Facebook Page or other social media accounts.

Maybe you do an article about changes to the tax laws for the new year that small businesses need to know about. That would be valuable information that you provide to the website visitors as well as your Facebook friends.

Every time you add a new article about taxes, it creates a new page for Google to show in search results. And it is something that hopefully your social media friends will share, helping spread your name.

## Content Updating

It is a very good idea to populate your website with new content on a regular basis. If you are a service company, this should be quite easy.

You're an accountant? Write articles about how to save money on your taxes.

So you're a mechanic? Write articles about how to best maintain the performance of your automobile.

Real estate agent? Write articles about what to look for in a new home or how to get your new home financed.

You get the idea. Whatever it is you do, you know stuff that other people would be interested in reading about.

My wife runs an antique store. She has had great success with before-and-after kind of articles. For instance, she might take an old desk, sand it down, then paint and distress it. The final product always ends up being quite beautiful compared to the original. And this, of course, ties in with items that you can buy at her store.

Certainly, anyone could read one of her articles, look at the pictures, and go and do the same thing herself. But one thing that the articles also demonstrate is the amount of work involved, and most people would just prefer to come buy one already made.

It is also a good idea to think in terms of keywords when coming up with article content. In other words, try to write articles about things that people are searching for online. Articles/blog posts are a great way to create keyword optimized content for your site, increasing the opportunities for generating search engine impressions for your website.

If you want to be really slick about it, what you could do is pre-plan a series of articles mapped to particular keywords and schedule them out in advance. We will talk more about keywords shortly.

In WordPress, you can set a blog post to appear at a later date. So you could go in and actually create the blog posts, set them to appear at certain dates, and then just leave them blank until you have a chance to get around to finishing the articles. If you do this, you need to make very sure that you actually do finish them before they get published. Otherwise, you will have a bunch of blank pages on your website.

## WordPress Configuration

There are a few things you will need to configure in your WordPress settings in order to give your website a better chance at ranking in search engines.

### Permalinks

Permalinks give your website URLs that are understandable by humans and search engines.

By default WordPress pages have URLs that consist of a ? followed by some variables. This is not good from a readability standpoint. It is a good idea for a human to be able to see the URL of the page and have a good understanding of what the page is about. Likewise, the URL is a place where you can place keywords for search engines.

To set up permalinks, go to Settings / Permalinks. I recommend setting it to "Post name," as shown below. What this means is that the title you give to a page or blog post will be used in the URL of the page.

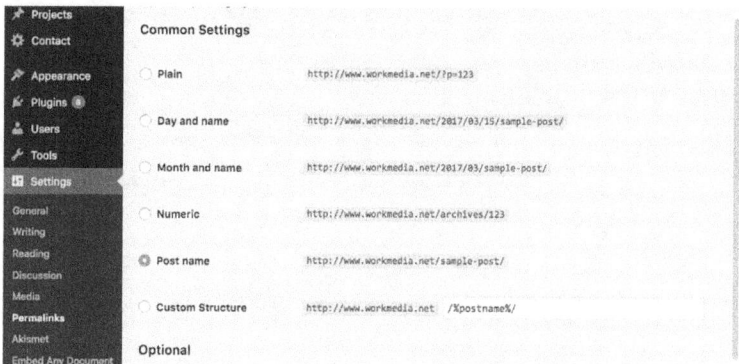

Another thing that I recommend you do is install an SEO plugin. There are a number of these, but one that I have used quite a bit is called Yoast SEO.

This discussion is based on the Yoast SEO plugin, but it should be a similar procedure for whatever particular plugin you use. On any given web page, there will be a place where you specify your target keyword for the page. Then the plugin will analyze the page to see if it is optimized adequately for your keyword.

As you tweak on the page to optimize it for your keyword, the plugin will give you feedback so you know if you have done what you need to do. For example, if your keyword is not contained in the page title or is not used enough in the copy, it will tell you that. Below is a screenshot to demonstrate what this looks like for a web page I optimized for the phrase "Kitec plumbing replacement."

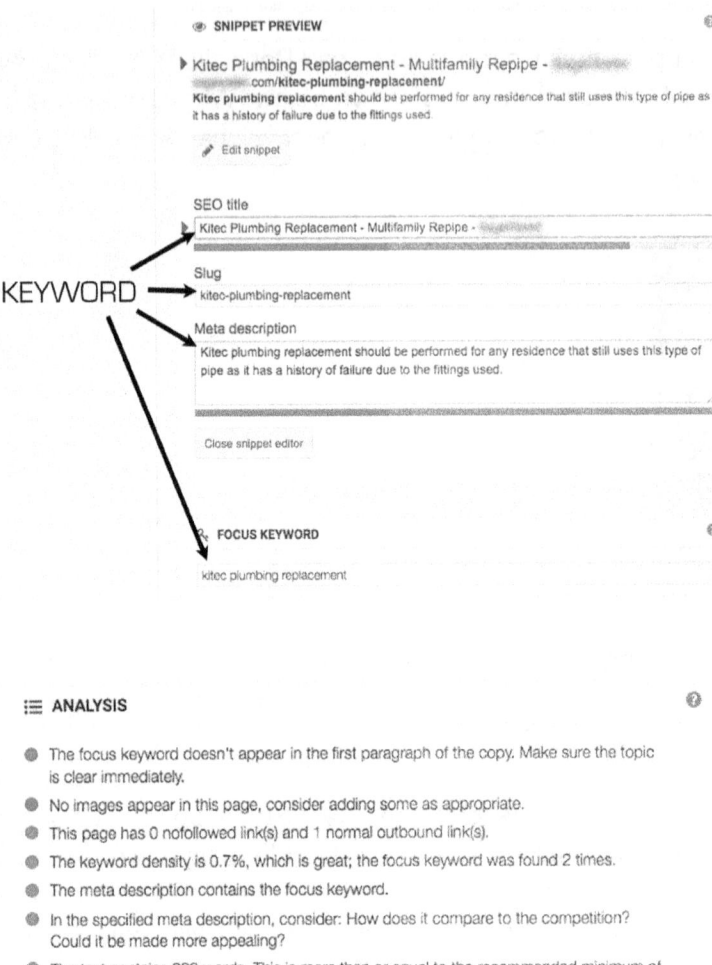

Basically, the plugin gives you your checklist of items you need to make sure you do on the page to optimize it for a particular keyword.

Shortly, we will get into the subject of on-page optimization, which will explain in more detail the items that the SEO plugin is checking.

# Search Engine Optimization

Now let's talk about SEO, which is how you get Google or other search engines to show your website in search listings when someone in your area searches for whatever it is you are selling (without paying for it).

## Keywords

Keywords are the words that people use to search the Web for a particular type of business or service. These words should be used strategically on your website to capture as much of that traffic as possible. A mistake that many business owners make is that they THINK they know what those words are, but they really don't.

Don't guess about what search terms someone might use to search for your type of business. Perform a process called keyword research to find out for sure what those words are. Google provides its own keyword research tool that will give you solid data to tell you what keywords you should be targeting.

### How to Do Keyword Research

Go to https://adwords.google.com/KeywordPlanner

You will need a Google AdWords account. Google AdWords is Google's advertising platform to allow you to pay for clicks to your website. You don't have to actually spend any money in this case. You just need to create an account so that you can gain access to the Keyword Planner tool.

There are also third party (non-Google) tools that will allow you to do keyword research, but I have always liked relying on Google's own data. Plus, it's free (unless you choose to run ads).

Once you are in Google AdWords, click Tools / Keyword Planner on the menu at the very top of the page to get to the keyword research tool.

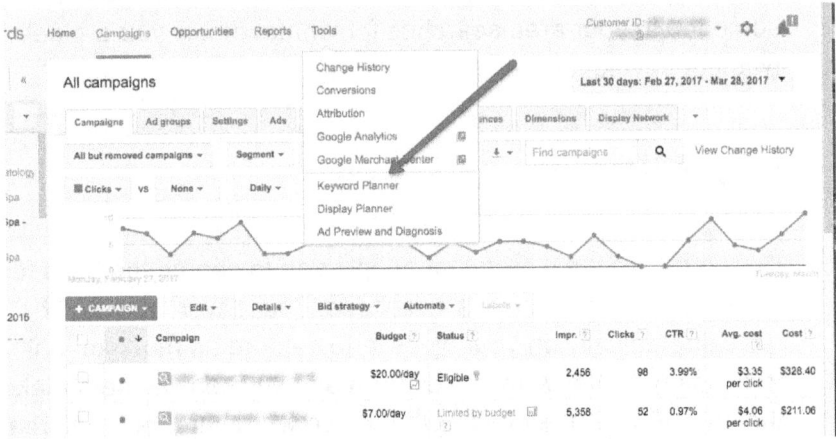

Click the box that says "Search for new keywords using a phrase, website or category." Then type in a few keywords related to your business.

There are also various options you can set such as running reports for a particular geographic area. If your business' market is a small town, then you may not return much data by selecting that as your market. If you do want to view data specific to your location, click the pencil icon next to "All locations" (in the section labeled "Targeting"). Then type a city, county, state or whatever you want in the textbox and click the blue Save button.

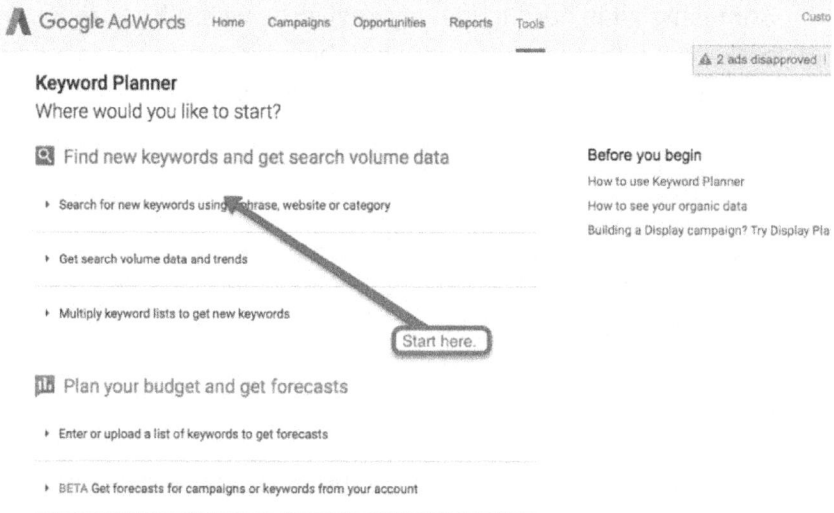

These Google screens change all the time, so chances are excellent that if you bought this book more than two days after I published it, it has changed. But it should be similar enough. Just look for the box where you type in words or phrases to get started.

The two main things you want to look for in your keywords are that they are highly relevant to your business and have some history of traffic. A third criteria is the competitiveness of the keywords. Obviously, the lower the competition, the better. You want to look for keywords that are very specific to your business. That will give you a better chance of ranking and a better chance of generating a conversion.

In other words, if you sell lumber in Dickson, Tennessee, you are much better off targeting a keyword like "Dickson TN lumber" than just "wood."

Traffic is the key. If you send me a list of 100 keywords with zero competition, I can have them all ranked number one in Google by next week. It would make the website owner feel good because he sees his website ranked in Google, but if those rankings don't actually drive any traffic to his website then he hasn't really accomplished anything.

Sometimes it is hard to identify keywords with a track record of clicks, so in that instance use your best judgment but focus on phrases that are highly relevant to your business.

Long tail versus high-volume

Keywords generally break out into two categories, and you should make use of both. The two types of keywords are high volume keywords and "long tail" keywords.

**High-volume**

These are the keywords that are most general and get the most traffic. These keywords are also usually very competitive. These keywords offer the possibility to drive a lot of traffic to your website but can be hard to get. They also don't convert as well.

**Long tail**

These are keywords that are much more specific. They will tend to be lower in volume than the keywords described above, but can be more profitable. They are easier to get and convert better.

Generally what you want to do his optimize your home page for the most broad, high volume keywords relevant to your business, but then optimize sub-pages of your site for the more specific long-tail keywords.

Let me give you an example.

Let's say you own a used car dealership in Dickson Tennessee. A high-volume keyword would be "used cars." A long, detailed keyword would be something like "Dickson Tennessee used car dealership."

"Used cars" could still be a good keyword if the business does a good job with its' local SEO, but we're not ready for that conversation yet.

The closer your webpage matches what the user is searching for, the better the chance you will do business with that person. This is called your conversion rate. If you have 100 visitors to your website and one of those visitors purchases from you or make some other kind of action, then that would be a 1% conversion rate (1 / 100).

However, if five of those 100 visitors make a purchase or some other action, then that is a 5% conversion rate. Long tail keywords tend to convert better, so even though they represent less traffic they can represent more sales.

So what's the next step after you have identified your keywords? At that point, you want to map those keywords to specific pages of your website, or build new pages for those keywords. You can't really optimize a web page for more than a couple of keywords. You've got to spread them out. I

Let's go back to our used car dealership example. Maybe one of his keywords is "Dickson Tennessee Chevrolet cars." That would make a good page for his site - a page specifically optimized for and about Chevrolet cars.

So now let's talk about how to actually optimize your website.

## On-page Optimization

The process of modifying a web pages title, copy and code so that the page has a better chance of ranking in a search engine is called on-page optimization. Here are the main things you need to know about it.

### Page URLs

Try to build out pages on your website that are optimized for specific keywords, and that use those keywords in the page URLs.

Let's say you are a company that provides a wide variety of data networking technologies in the Nashville area. A good URL for a page about the installation of closed caption television systems would be something like "/nashville-closed-caption-tv/."

Having the primary keyword for a web page in the URL for that page can help it rank for that keyword. Try to build out a catalog of pages on your website optimized for a variety of keywords, with the keywords in the URLs. Publishing a regular blog is a good way to do this. Using the Permalinks feature of WordPress also helps accomplish this goal because a page will automatically have a URL that contains the page title.

## Page Titles

The page title is the single most important thing about a web page as far as ranking in a search engine like Google. Use your main keyword for a page in the page title. If it makes sense, start the title with the keyword.

Say the name of a used tire dealer is "Jack's Tire Shop." A good title for his website home page would be something like "McEwen Tennessee Tires – New and Used – Jack's Tire Shop." This page would have a good chance at ranking for the keyword phrase "McEwen Tennessee tires" just because that exact keyword phrase is used in the title.

This needs to be done on every major page of your website, not just your home page.

## Copy

Next, you should try to use the keyword a couple of times in the copy on the page. Also try to use it in a header (text inside <H1> tags). There are three SEO criteria to keep in mind when writing your copy: word count, keyword density, and keyword prominence.

## Word Count

This is just the total number of words in the copy. Generally speaking, more copy is better. Aim for a minimum of 300 words. If you can hit 500, especially on content-rich sub-pages, that is even better. If you can hit 1,000 words, that is dynamite.

## Keyword Density

This is the number of times a keyword appears in the copy divided by the total number of words in the copy. Aim for a keyword density of 1%. But avoid making it appear artificial.

## Keyword Prominence

This is how near the top of the copy your keyword appears. If you can make your keyword phrase the very first words on the page, that is great. But again, it should sound natural, and not forced. Try to get your keyword into the first paragraph or two if you can.

You are trying to give Google lots of clues as to what the page is about. If the page is about a Dickson Tennessee tire dealer, then you need to make that very clear to Google.

## Meta Tags

After you have created a good title and copy for the page, the next step is to write a good meta description. This is basically a short paragraph that represents what Google will say about your website in the search results (although it doesn't have to use the meta description - sometimes it will just use text from the page).

The meta description is another thing that can influence how Google ranks your website, so it should be optimized for your target keyword for the page. However, it should read like a human written paragraph.

This process should be done on every major page of the site. Each page is optimized for one or two specific keywords.

## Cross-linking

Try to sprinkle keyword links throughout the copy in the various pages. In other words, if our used car dealer has a page on his site devoted to trucks and a page devoted to cars, the truck page might have a link to the car page with the words "used cars." This process is called "cross linking."

Let's look at another hypothetical example to give you a more clear idea of what we're talking about.

Let's say you own a small bookkeeping business in a little town called Centerville. You would need to do keyword research to identify what your top keyword should be. But it's probably safe to assume that your core number one keyword would be something like "Centerville bookkeeping service."

In this case, you would want to have elements on your homepage similar to the following.

Page title: Centerville Bookkeeping Service – Small Business Accounting

At the top of the page, your keyword would be contained in a header, like this:

<H1>Centerville bookkeeping Service</H1>

The phrase "Centerville bookkeeping service" would be contained within the first paragraph or two of copy and would be in bold, like this:

<Strong >Centerville bookkeeping service </strong >

You would also want the keyword to be contained near the bottom of the copy on the page.

Try to have a minimum of 300 words in the main copy of the page, with your keyword used two to three times.

You will also need to use your keyword in the meta description for the page. That will look something like this:

<meta name = "description" content = "Centerville bookkeeping service – small business accounting for middle Tennessee"/>

As you can see, the meta-description is very similar to the page title, but is a little longer, allowing you to put in a little more detail. The meta description would appear in the head of the HTML document, and not in the body copy. It is not seen by the visitor.

The tags that you see around the information above (such as "title" used around the page title) are called HTML tags. One of the big advantages of using a platform like WordPress is that it is a WYSIWYG ("what you see is what you get") editor, meaning you can edit the content of your webpages without knowing HTML.

Now let's take a step back.

So what you have done above is optimize one page of your website for one keyword. However, it is very unlikely that all of the potential customers for your business will use the exact same keyword phrase. People think differently. They will use different words to search for your type of business.

But you don't have to just guess about that. Refer back to the section of this book about keyword research for details about how to use Google to find out what keywords people actually use to search for your type of business.

Keywords that are very similar or that sort of cross over, can be used on the same page. For example, the three keywords below would all fit nicely into the page described above:

Centerville bookkeeping service
Bookkeeping service
Centerville bookkeeping

This is pretty typical of the way keywords can fit together at times.

For keywords that are very different, you will need to optimize a separate page for those keywords. Maybe our bookkeeping service also specializes in managing books for clients who use QuickBooks. If people are searching using the phrase "QuickBooks bookkeeping service," then it would be a good idea for our hypothetical bookkeeper to have a separate page on his or her website optimized for that phrase.

So let's go through the same exercise as above.

Page title: Centerville QuickBooks Bookkeeping Service – Small Business

Header: Centerville QuickBooks Bookkeeping Service

Meta-Description: Centerville QuickBooks bookkeeping service for small businesses in the middle Tennessee area. 20 years of experience.

And so the process continues. I often call this "keyword mapping" because you are essentially mapping keywords to specific pages of your site. If there are highly relevant, good traffic keywords that don't correspond to any page of your site, you will need to create page from scratch. This is something I do often because it is a way to capture a far greater share of the overall search traffic relative to your business.

## Site Maps

A site map is a page or file on your website that has a link to every page (or most pages). There are two types of site maps: HTML and XML.

### HTML

An HTML site map is a publicly accessible page of your site that has links to all the other pages (or at least the pages you want people to find). This page is helpful both for humans as well as search engines. For your human visitors, it is just a quick way for them to find whatever page has the information they are looking for. For search engines, it makes it easier for them to explore the site and make a record of all the pages.

If you use WordPress for your site, you can install a plugin that will create your site map for you. However, as a word of warning, sometimes things get added to an automatically generated site map that you don't really want on there. Depending on how your WordPress theme works, there could be things that are actually parts of a page that the site map would consider a complete page. Make sure your sitemap only has links to legitimate pages that you want people and search engines to find.

### XML

XML site maps are really just for search engines. XML is a markup language kind-of like HTML, but it is generally not really used as the main scripting language of a webpage. If you are using WordPress, you can install a plugin that will generate your XML site map for you.

In the section of this book about Google Webmaster, we go into detail about how to submit your XML site map to Google.

## Links

The other side of SEO is creating links and building social media credibility for your website.

You need some links from other websites pointing to your website. The higher the quality of the link, the more it helps you.

A good place to start is an industry directory related to whatever it is you sale. In our used car example, if there is a website devoted to lists of used car dealerships in the United States, then we should have a listing in that directory with a link back to our website.

Another great way to get a link is to write an article about your industry and submit it for inclusion on another website along with a link back to your website.

Having other websites link to your website is one factor that plays into your search engine ranking. All else equal, a website that has more or better quality links pointing to it will rank better. But quality is more important than quantity. If you can get CNN.com to link to your website, that is a very valuable link.

Of course, to get a link like that, your website needs to be associated with some kind of big time national story, or you need to be prepared to spend many thousands of dollars for the link. For the small business, it is just not feasible, so you will have to start with the basics and then use your creativity to find sources of links.

One strategy is to look at the link sources for your top online competitors, or any companies in your industry with good search engine visibility.

Here is a free tool that you can use to discover some competitor links:

https://moz.com/researchtools/ose/

Type in the competitor website address and then look through the links for possible websites where you might also be able to get a link.

## Trust flow

For a number of years there was a concept very important in the search engine optimization process called "PageRank." PageRank is a sort-of ranking of importance that Google applies to web pages. What was useful about it is that that value could be passed around from one web page to another. So getting links from high PageRank web pages helped improve search rankings of the web page that is being linked to.

At the time of this writing, PageRank has given way to another concept called "Trust Flow." The idea behind Trust Flow is basically that you want websites to link to your website, and you want to link out to other websites, that are legitimate and highly relevant to the subject of your website.

If you sell neon signs, you should try to get links from other web pages that relate to signs, neon, advertising, whatever. And you should also have links on your website to other websites related to the same thing. You want to make it clear to Google that your website is devoted to the subject of neon signs by being a trusted flow of information on that subject.

Links from higher quality websites carry more weight and help improve your ranking more than lesser quality sites. Quality is more important than quantity.

Let's consider a CPA based in Bellevue, Tennessee. After optimizing his website for relevant keywords uncovered through keyword research, the next thing he would want to do is add some links from his site to other high quality, relevant web pages that feature content related to accounting or financial topics.

Next, you need to try and get some links pointing to your website from other websites in your industry. This can be more tricky. The easiest way to start is with any kind of industry directory you can find. For our CPA, this would be directories related to accounting, bookkeeping or other financial service type businesses.

Over the years, a number of tactics were devised to create links. These included things like publishing articles on article directories, adding your site to social bookmarking accounts, and submitting online press releases. Google has greatly decreased the value of these tactics. The main thing to keep in mind is that you want links from and to other websites that focus on a topic that is relevant to your website.

## Your Domain Name

Your domain name represents your address on the web. There are two general approaches to web domain names: branded domain versus keyword domain. By this time, most really good keyword ".com" domains are already taken. If you can't find a .com, try a .net. Spend some time searching for a really great domain name. If you find more than one, you can register multiple domains and redirect them all to the same location.

At this point, I do still believe it is better to go with a .com domain, with .net being my second choice. These days there are lots of alternatives, but .com and .net remain the easiest for most people to remember.

There are lots of registrars of domain names, so it doesn't really matter where you go to purchase your domain. GoDaddy.com is a one popular registrar that has good prices. They also offer hosting, although that is another area where there are lots of good options.

Your website designer is a good resource for help getting a good domain name registered for your website.

## Google Webmaster

You are going to need to set up a Google WebMaster account. This will give you some control over how Google finds and displays your website, as well as providing some valuable information that can help you with your website marketing.

To create your account, go to
https://www.google.com/webmasters.

If you don't already have a Google account, you will need to set one up. If you do already have a Google account, just click the sign in button. Once you are logged in to Google, visit the link above. To add your website, click the add a property button.

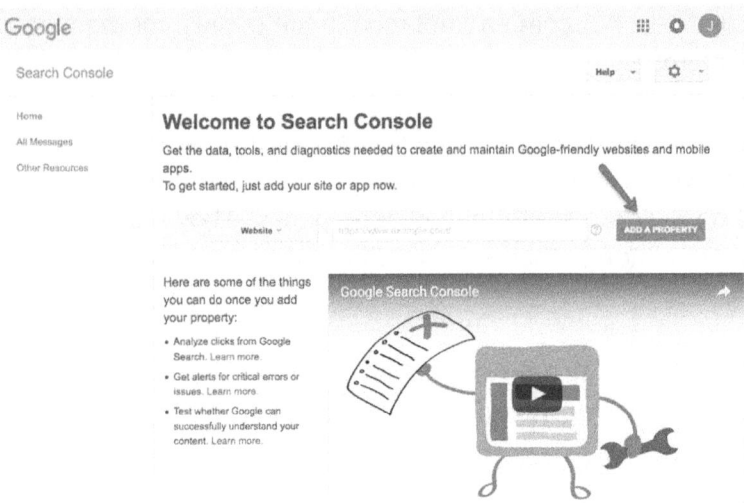

Before Google will allow you to use its WebMaster functionality, you have to prove that you are the owner or manager of the website. There are a few different ways that Google allows you to do this, but the quickest way is to upload a file that Google provides to your server. Then when Google finds the file, it knows that you have control of the site and are qualified to act as its Webmaster.

After getting your account set up, the first thing you should do is submit an XML sitemap. To do that, go to the Crawl/Sitemaps page and click the Add/Test Sitemap button. You will then provide the URL to your website sitemap. Which means, obviously, that there has to be an XML sitemap.

The easiest way to get that added to your website is to use a WordPress plugin. There is one called Google Sitemap Generator that is popular. If you don't use WordPress and don't have any way to automatically created a sitemap, you can create one manually using any text editor. Unless you are a real nerd, I would look for an automated way to do it.

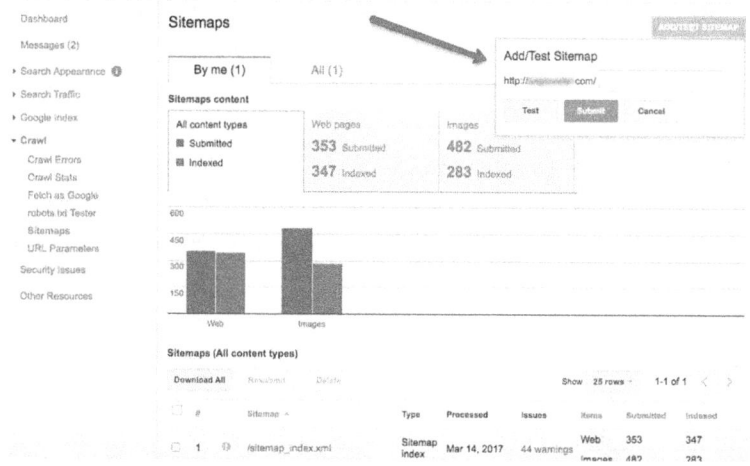

Two things that Google shows you in your WebMaster account that are very useful to know are Google search impressions and clicks. It will also show you a list of keywords that were used in Google that resulted in impressions or clicks to your website.

It will show you your average ranking for the keyword and the click-through rate. If you see promising keywords in the list where your ranking is not that great, then those might be good candidates for SEO.

To clarify, an impression is when someone loads a search engine results page that has your website in the listings. An impression does not necessarily mean that the visitor clicked to your website. But you can't have clicks until you have impressions.

Google will not show you a complete list of all the keywords that generated impressions or clicks. I believe the general rule is that it won't show search phrases that consist of more than five words, but don't hold me to it. The point is that Google will show you many of the keywords people are using to find your website, but not all of them.

Your Google WebMaster account is also where you submit your XML site map. Go to the Crawl/Site Maps page and click the button to add your site map. You will then give Google the URL to

45

your site map page. After some period of time, Google will process the site map and tell you if there were any problems with it.

Another important thing that Google will tell you is if it has had any crawl errors on your site. These are errors that Google has encountered while traveling through your site. You should work to fix these.

For example, if Google finds links on some pages that are incorrect, it will tell you. The cleaner your website is in terms of bad links or other mistakes, the better your chances of ranking well.

## Website Load Speed

The faster a browser is able to load your website, the better.

There are lots of different ways to increase how fast your website loads. I'm not going to get into a lot of them because some of it is pretty technical stuff. But two things that I will talk about here that you should know about are file caching and image compression.

File caching is a process whereby your web pages are stored somewhere in memory, either on the website server or on your own computer. The reason caching is useful for speeding up your website is that the server does not have to take the time to construct the web pages from all the different little pieces.

A web page is typically made up of all these different files that the server puts together to create the code that it sends to your computer or mobile device via the Internet. So if rather than having to go through that whole process, the server can just send you an HTML file that is all ready to go, that causes your web page to load quicker.

Image compression is the act of reducing the file size of the images on your website. The best way to do this is to reduce the file size yourself before you ever upload an image to the website. However, there are also plugins and such that will perform this as well.

There are a number of online tools you can use to test your website speed. Here are a few:

- https://developers.google.com/speed/pagespeed/insights/

- https://gtmetrix.com/

- http://www.speedtest.net/

It is a good idea to test your site with more than one tool and compare the results. If the results show that your website is too slow, then the problem could be any combination of the following issues:

- Poor performing website hosting.

- Too many plugins or other extra "stuff."

- Graphics that are too large.

- Not making use of any kind of caching.

Website load speed is even more important on mobile devices. More and more search traffic comes from mobile devices, and if Google detects that your site is too slow, it will not show it in mobile search results.

There are a million different reasons why your website might be slow to load. If you can't figure it out, you might want to hire some help to solve the problem.

## Mobile Friendliness

Your website must be mobile friendly. This is not an option. It is a necessity.

If I have to scroll to the side to read your website on my phone, you have a problem.

If it takes forever for your website to load on my phone, you have a problem.

If I have to squint to read your website on my phone because the text is so small, you have a problem.

It could be more important for your website to be mobile friendly than it is to be optimized. There is evidence that Google is moving toward ranking sites based on mobile friendliness and load time above sites that just work well on a desktop computer. Look at your website on your phone. Make sure it is easy to read and navigate.

### AMP

AMP, which stands for "Accelerated Mobile Pages," is a brand new technology that can greatly improve the mobile user experience. What it does is send a stripped down, super fast version of a web page for mobile viewing. Google is able to detect if you have AMP installed, and it automatically links mobile search results to the AMP version of your site.

If you use WordPress, this is easily accomplished with use of an AMP plugin. When I first started testing this technology in WordPress, it worked perfectly the first time on two out of three websites. On the third one, it didn't cause any problems, but for some reason Google was unable to detect AMP.

If you don't use WordPress or some other platform where some smart people have already created something that will do AMP for you, then this is probably above your head. WordPress makes it easy.

## Ranking Tracking

It is useful to track your rankings for your target keywords over time. Combined with your organic search traffic statistics, this will paint the picture if you are making progress in improving your search engine visibility.

It is not my intention to promote any particular third-party service, especially since I'm not making money from it, but I might as will mention MOZ.com as a good option for tracking your rankings. It is probably the number one service for this.

The way any ranking tracking service works is that it is going to periodically perform a Google search for each of your target keywords to see where it ranks. Generally this happens once per week. You can also specify if you want to track rankings on a nationwide basis or from a particular geographic area.

MOZ will also integrate with your Google analytics to display traffic statistics from organic search. It is convenient to have that data in the same interface as your search engine ranking data, because it sort of ties everything together. What you should see is that as your rankings improve, your organic search traffic improves as well.

MOZ is a paid service, and although extremely useful for someone like me who does this stuff all the time, it is not mandatory. If you want, you can just go to Google once per week and type your target keywords in yourself to see where you rank.

Word of caution: if you are logged into Google when you do this, your results will be distorted because Google will tailor the search results to your search history. So to get more accurate ranking results if doing this yourself, you need to make sure you're logged out of Google. The process of manually tracking the rankings can be a real pain, especially if you're tracking a large number of keywords. That's why it is convenient to you to use an automated service that does it for you once per week. Or if you have a teenager, maybe you can put him or her to work on the task.

# Local SEO

When it comes to businesses that operate in a limited geographic market, things are done a little differently. This is a specific type of SEO called "local SEO."

The key components to a local SEO campaign are:

- Optimizing your website for local.

- Managing your Google Business account.

- Creating citations.

- Getting reviews.

## Local Optimization

The whole point of local optimization is to make it very clear to Google that you are a legitimate business, what your business is, and where you are located. To accomplish these goals, do this:

- Use your page titles, meta descriptions and copy to make it very clear what your business is, as described in the on-page optimization section above.

- Put the street address and phone number in your website footer.

- Have a contact / location page on your site with your address and a Google map.

- If you have more than one location, each location should have its own page with complete contact information.

# Google Business

A Google Business account is your key to getting your website to show up in the local section of a Google search results page, as shown below:

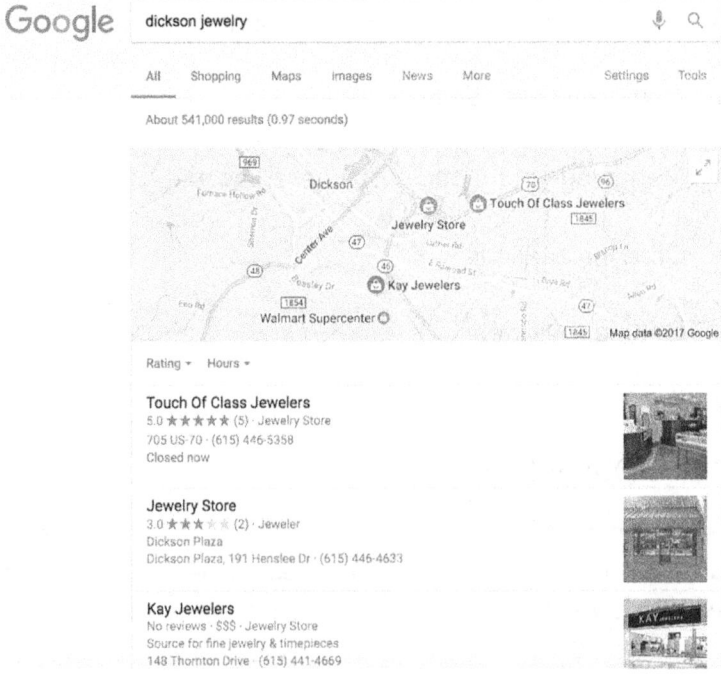

Google pulls that local business information from businesses that have Google Business accounts. If you don't have one, you're not going to show up.

Set up a Google business page by going to:

https://business.google.com/create

If you don't already have a Google account, that is step one. Click the Create account link and just follow the instructions to create a Google account.

Once your Google account is created, you will arrive at a welcome screen that has a blue button that says "Continue to Google My Business." If you don't see that button, use the web address shown above to get to the Google Business signup page.

The first page of the signup process is where you start telling Google all about your business - your name, address, phone, category, etc. Be very careful to type in all of your information correctly. The information you type in here should match what is shown on your website.

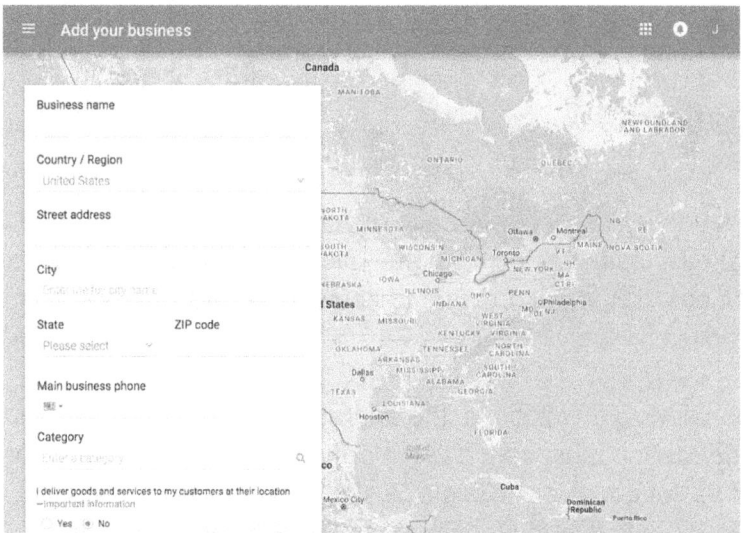

Google will then attempt to display your business address on a map and require you to click a button stating that you are authorized to manage the business and agree to Google's terms.

To complete the process, you will need a verification code that you get via a postcard from Google.

While you wait on the postcard from Google, you should go ahead and start filling out the details of your Google Business page. Use every option there is. Give your page a header background. Provide hours of operation, your website address and a phone number.

Add as many photos as it will let you. Even if your business doesn't necessarily lend itself to photography, find a reason to take some pictures anyway.

Once your page is verified, which you can do after you receive the Google postcard, your business will be eligible to appear in Google local search results.

So now that you have a Google Business account set up with information that matches what is on your website, the next step is to start setting up some citations.

## Citations

A citation is simply a reference to your business in some kind of local business directory or portal, along with an address for your business. It is very important to have these for local SEO purposes.

When setting up citations, the address and phone number shown in the citation must match the information shown on your website and as set up in your Google Business account. You need to make it very clear to Google exactly where you are located.

## Local Directories

Here are some of the top websites at which you should add your business:

- www.Yelp.com
- www.BingPlaces.com
- www.CitySearch.com

- www.HotFrog.com
- www.YellowPages.com
- www.SuperPages.com
- www.Foursquare.com

Visit all of these websites and add your business. I would probably start with Yelp.

## Yelp

To get your business listed in Yelp, you first have to see if it is in the Yelp directory, and then "claim" it if it is. To do that, go to the bottom of the page at https://www.yelp.com and click the link that says "Claim Your Business Page."

On the next page, type your business name in the appropriate box, make sure the correct city is selected, and click the Get Started button.

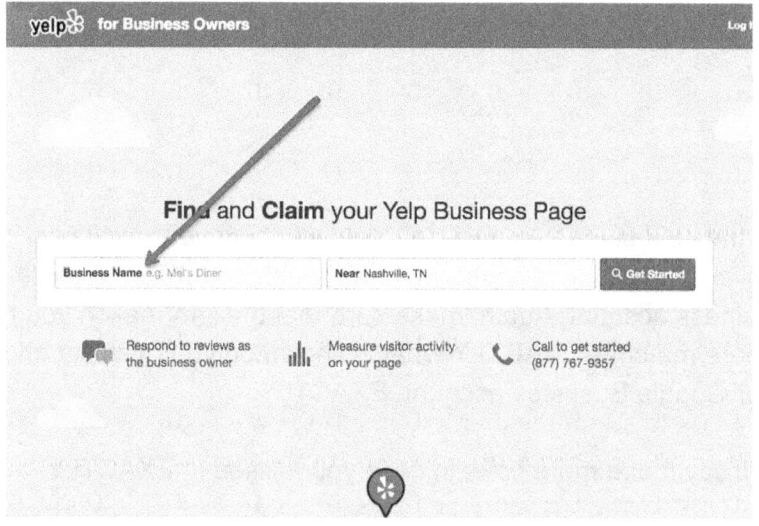

If you don't find your business, then at the bottom of the list of businesses that Yelp shows you on the next page, click the link that says "Add your business to Yelp."

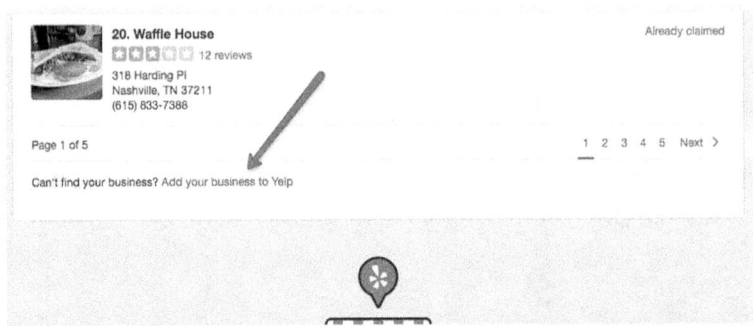

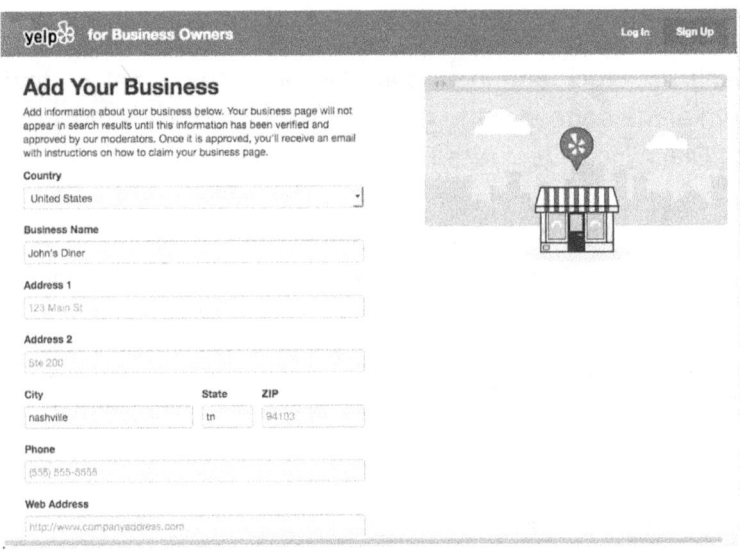

On the next screen, you will tell Yelp all about your business, similar to what you did when you were setting up your Google Business account. Again, make sure that the information you type in here matches EXACTLY what is shown on your website and in your Google Business account. EXACTLY.

I will say it one more time, in case you missed it: EXACTLY.

The process for signing up at the other local directory sites will vary. Some of them will require verification similar to Google. In some of them, like Yelp, your business could already be in the site, in which case you will have to claim it.

The above list is nowhere near a complete list of local directories, but if you start with this list, that will give you a real good start. If you add to this list over time, you will increase your total citations, thus helping improve your search rankings and potentially exposing your business to many new prospects.

I have not spent a whole lot of time on this section, as I leave it up to you to explore the above list of local portals. But do not overlook this. Creating citations is especially important for businesses operating at a local level.

# Reviews

Google gives preference to business websites that have reviews. I would recommend that you try to get reviews at least two places: Your Google Business profile and your Yelp profile.

If you have a really lousy business and regularly cheat your customers, you will probably have reviews start popping up organically. It's not very hard to get negative reviews. Most people who go out of their way to talk about a business are doing so because they are unhappy.

To get positive reviews, you are going to need to ask your happy customers to review your business. I recommend giving them very specific instructions. I recommend giving them instructions similar to what follows.

### Instructions for Leaving Social Media Reviews

We greatly appreciate you taking the time to follow these instructions to review our business online.

**Google**

Instructions for leaving a Google review:

1. Visit https://www.google.com. If you are not logged into Google, click the Sign In button in the upper right-hand corner.

2. If you do not have a Google account, follow the easy instructions to create one. Otherwise, type in your password to log into Google.

3. After logging in, do a Google search for "[your business name]."

4. On the right side of the screen, click the "Write a review" button.

5. Assign us a star rating (we would certainly appreciate 5!) and a comment in the "Describe your experience" section. Then click POST.

**Yelp**

Instructions for leaving a Yelp review:

1. Visit https://www.yelp.com/biz/[your Yelp business page].

2. Click the red Write a Review button.

3. On the next screen, leave us a number of stars and a review.

4. Click the red Sign Up and Post button and follow the instructions from there.

## Local Offers

Getting a new customer can be difficult. One strategy that can work well for any business, but especially businesses operating at a local level, is the free consultation. Some how, some way, you need to get people to your business, even if you have to bribe them.

You need to think of customer generation in terms of a funnel. There are likely many hundreds or thousands of prospective customers in your market area. So the first thing you have to do is make those people aware that you exist. The next thing you have to do is get as many of those people as you can to contact your business.

Some of those people who contact your business will become customers. Many will not. This is why it's called a "funnel." Lots of people will enter the top of your funnel but only so many will become customers. The more people you pour into that funnel, the more customers will come out the other end.

So as I mentioned above, one way to feed the top of the funnel is to offer something for free. Free legal consultation. Free oil change. Free report. Free donuts. Free poster. Free sample. Whatever.

Often, it is a good idea to have a sort of multi-tiered approach to whatever it is you sale. You might want to have some kind of low-cost product or service to start with. Or maybe you give a big discount to first-time customers.

It is way more expensive to sell to a new customer then it is to someone who is already a customer. So it is perfectly fine to make less money, or possibly even lose money, to get the customer to start with. You can make much more selling to that customer long-term.

# Paid Search

So let's talk about paid search, also called "pay per click." You have probably noticed that if you do a search on Google, there are some listings at the top that have a little "ad" icon next to them. Those are paid ads. When someone clicks on one of those listings, that business is charged a fee for that click.

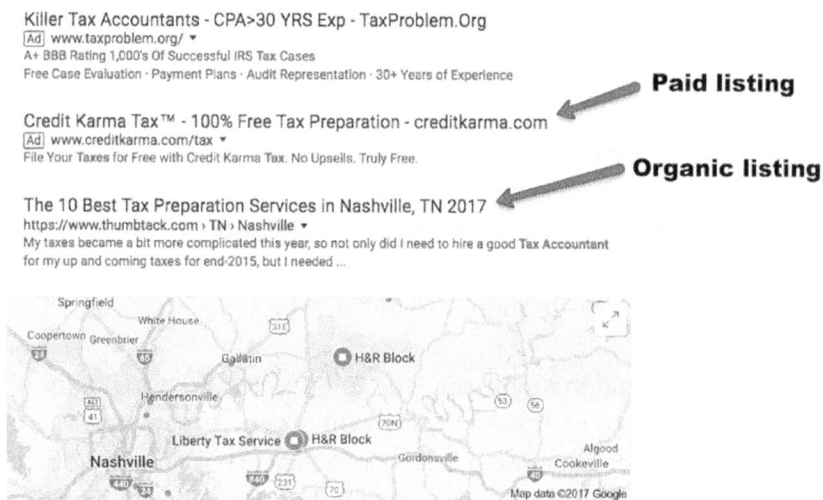

There are a couple of reasons you might want to pay for clicks. For one, it takes time to get your website in the organic listings. It can take months. Also, if you have both organic and paid listings on a search results page, that increases your search engine "shelf space." We'll talk about shelf space later.

The two major paid search platforms are Google AdWords and Bing Ads. Google obviously gets the most traffic, but Bing is worth trying as well and you might even save some money.

Now there are a few important concepts you need to understand.

## Cost per Cilck

This is the amount of money you pay for one click. It won't be the same for every keyword, and it won't be the same every day. Paid search is basically an auction model where you bid a certain amount you are willing to pay for a click. However, your bid is not the only thing that determines when and where your ad will show up. Where your ad shows up is a function of many things, but some of the main things are:

- How much you bid for the keyword.

- How much competition there is for the keyword.

- How relevant the keyword is to its landing page.

- The click-through-rate of the ad.

Back in the olden days you used to be able to get clicks for a nickel. There ain't no nickel clicks anymore. These days, some businesses are spending $50+ on a click. That seems absurd, but it's not about the click cost - it's about your return on investment (discussed earlier) and cost per conversion (discussed below).

## Cost per Conversion

Cost per conversion is what it costs you in dollars to get one conversion. A conversion does not necessarily have to be a sale, but for our purposes here let's just assume that it is. So if a law firm spends $1,000 on Google AdWords, and that generates 5 clients, then the cost per conversion would be $200.

The trick to knowing that is knowing how many sales the AdWords ads actually generated, which can be tricky when selling real world products off-line. But you get the idea. Cost per conversion is calculated by dividing how much you spent in advertising by the number of sales the advertising generated.

Cost per conversion is very close related to return on investment.

If you spend $100 on Google AdWords clicks, and as a result make $500 in sales, then you have a return on investment of 400% ($4 in profit for every $1 spent in advertising).

# Google AdWords

To get started with Google AdWords, visit https://adwords.google.com.

You will first have to log in with your Google account. If you don't have a Google account… have you been paying attention? Go sign up for a Google account… NOW!

WARNING: Google is very good at getting your money. If you don't know what you're doing, you can spend a lot and not get much out of it. Be careful. Work with an AdWords professional if you don't feel comfortable with this stuff.

## Campaigns and Ad Groups

Your AdWords account will divide out into logical groupings called campaigns and ad groups. A campaign consists of ad groups. An ad group is a combination of keywords and ads.

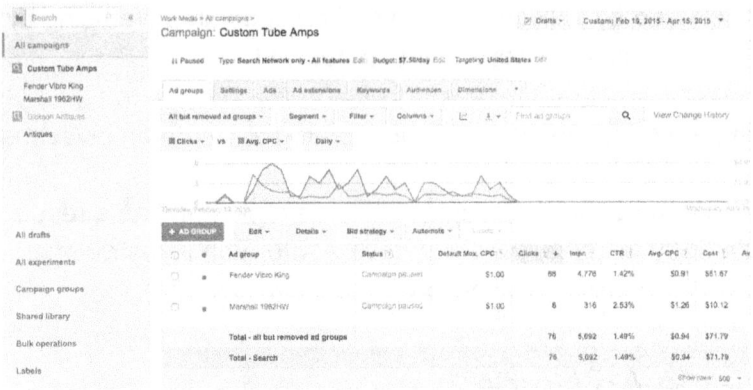

All of the ads and keywords in a particular ad group should be very related. For example, our auto dealer's AdWords account might have a Ford ad group that contains keywords and ads that reference Ford vehicles. Or maybe it's even more specific than that and is about Ford Mustangs.

The more closely related an ad is to the exact information the searcher is looking for, the more effective it will be. So if the person is looking for a Ford truck...show him an ad about Ford Trucks. And link the ad to a page on your website about Ford trucks.

The campaign level is a higher level up than ad groups and represents a broader grouping. For example, our car dealer might have a truck campaign and a car campaign. Or maybe it's a Ford campaign and a Chevy campaign, depending on how he breaks things out. Then each of those campaigns would break down into models or type of vehicle.

Budgets are set at the campaign level. So shifting budget for one set of keywords to another usually involves using different campaigns. Say our car dealer notices that his car ads are performing a lot better than his truck ads. Having trucks and cars in different campaigns would allow him to shift budget toward cars so that he is spending more money where he's getting the best return on investment.

Your geographic targeting also happens at the campaign level. So if you need to allocate separate budgets for different geographic markets or target those markets with different ads, then you will need to use separate campaigns for those markets.

There are a number of different ways to tell Google how much you want to pay for each click. You can let Google set your bids for you if you specify that you want to get as many clicks as you can within your budget. In that case, Google will automatically move bids up and down to accomplish that goal. Sometimes this works well. However, there have been times when I was very unsatisfied with the results I got from this technique. So at that point I would just set the bids myself manually.

Another thing that I have found about letting Google set bids is that Google tends to bid for very high positioning – ads that appear in the top one or two positions. This can be expensive. You can get lower cost clicks by bidding for lower positions.

Starting out, what you might want to do is set your bids to a level at which you are comfortable and then make adjustments over time as you go.

Google can also adjust your bids based on conversion data. This actually brings me to an important topic, which is that you can be much more effective with paid search (and all marketing) if you have a way to track conversions. So let's talk about it.

## Conversion Tracking

You need to know when someone visits your site and takes some kind of action. That action can be filling out a contact form, calling you on the phone, or making a purchase.

The contact form conversion can be tracked using a conversion tracking code that Google will supply you. In order for this to work, when someone submits the contact form on your site, she needs to be redirected to a thank you page. That is where the conversion tracking code is located. This allows Google to tell you when that form was filled out by someone who arrived from a paid click.

To find the conversion tracking script, click Tools/Conversions on the top main menu. Then click the +Conversion button.

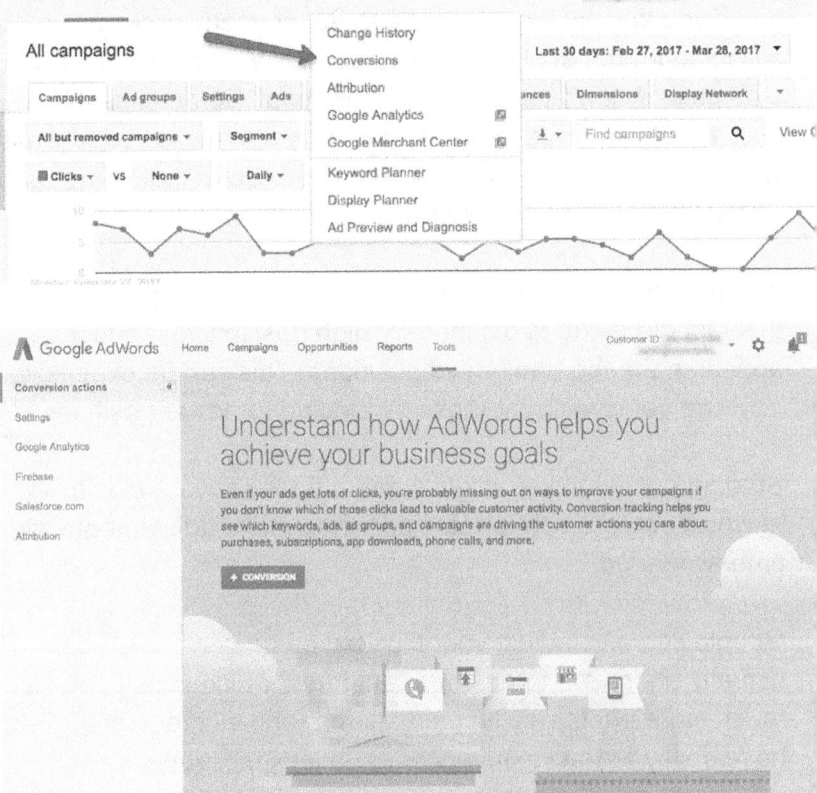

There are a few different types of conversions you can track, but the two you will likely use are Website conversions (form submissions or online sales) and Phone calls (when someone calls you after seeing your ad).

For phone conversions, you will need a call tracking number. This is a phone number that is different from your main number but redirects to your business. This allows you to track conversions because you will know that those calls originated from your AdWords click.

Select the type of conversion you want to track and follow the instructions. There are a lot of different options here and ways to set up your conversions. I don't really want to bog down this book with a lot of technical instructions on setting up conversions. Again, if you're not sure what you're doing, consult the help of an AdWords pro.

## Geographic Targeting

You need to tell Google exactly where you want your ad to run. If you own a barbecue restaurant in Bellevue, Tennessee, then you want your ad to appear when someone in Bellevue, Tennessee searches for "barbecue." It doesn't help you for your ad to appear in New York City.

Even if you don't really have a limited market area, it is probably unrealistic for you to promote your website nationwide unless you have a very specific product or service that is marketed to a very limited group of people.

Your target market is set in the campaign settings. This allows you to run different campaigns in different markets. This is one way to fine-tune your ads to people in particular locations.

## Keywords

Keywords are the search terms that should trigger your ads. For example, if you own a flower shop in Jackson, Tennessee, you might use keywords like:

Flower shop
Flowers
Buy flowers
Jackson flower shop

So when someone who is in the Jackson area searches Google for one of these keywords (or something very similar), he would see your ad. How closely the search query has to match the keyword is determined by the keyword match type.

## Match Types

The keyword match type determines how closely the user's search query must match the keyword in your account in order for Google to show your ad.

The three main types of keyword match types are:

- Exact match
- Broad match
- Phrase much

### Exact Match

Exact match means that Google will only show your ad if the search query used matches your keyword exactly. This is the safest kind of match type to use. However, you may end up limiting the number of times your ad appears.

### Broad Match

Broad match means that Google will show your ad if the search query is similar to, but not necessarily the same as, your keyword. Using broad match keywords may greatly increase the number of times your ad appears in search results, but it can also result in many more non-relevant matches.

### Phrase Match

Phrase much means that the user's search query must contain your keyword exactly as it is, but can also have additional words before or after it. If the keyword is "tractor sales", then the search queries "Jackson tractor sales" and "tractor sales auction" would both trigger the ad.

So what type of match type should you use for the keywords in your account? I usually like to start with mostly exact match. And then if I'm just not getting enough traffic, I will begin adding broad match or phrase match keywords as well.

One strategy I have used a lot is to have each keyword in my account set as both exact match and broad match. If there is an exact match on the keyword, then that is the match that Google should make. I should get the best click cost with an exact match. However, if the user uses a similar but not exactly the same keyword, then you can still capture that traffic with the broad match keyword.

Google will show you the exact search phrases that have resulted in clicks. So what you can do is go through that list periodically and add attractive phrases as keywords in your account if they are not already. To see this information, click Dimensions, then change the View dropdown list to "Search terms."

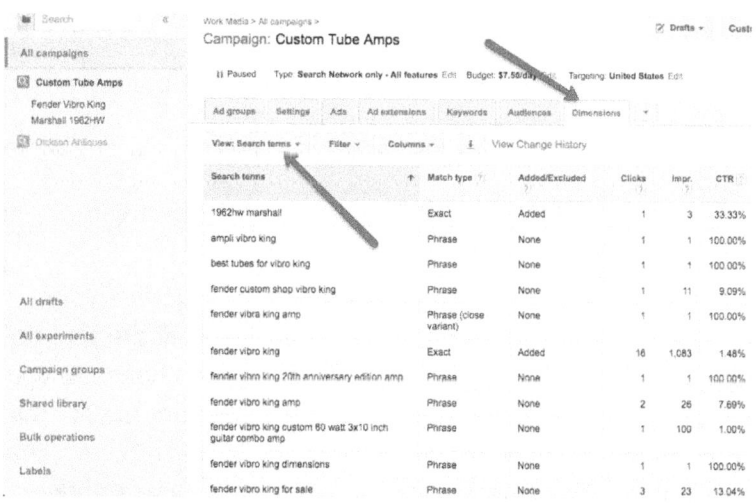

# Dayparting

Another way you can fine-tune your account is to only run ads at certain times of the day. This is called dayparting. Initially, it will be difficult to know if there is any advantage to doing this. What you want to do is look at your data over time to see if you have better performance at certain times of day, and then start running ads more during those times.

Similarly, you may find that it is more productive to run ads on certain days of the week. Or maybe you want to decrease your click cost on the weekend. These are all things that can be adjusted.

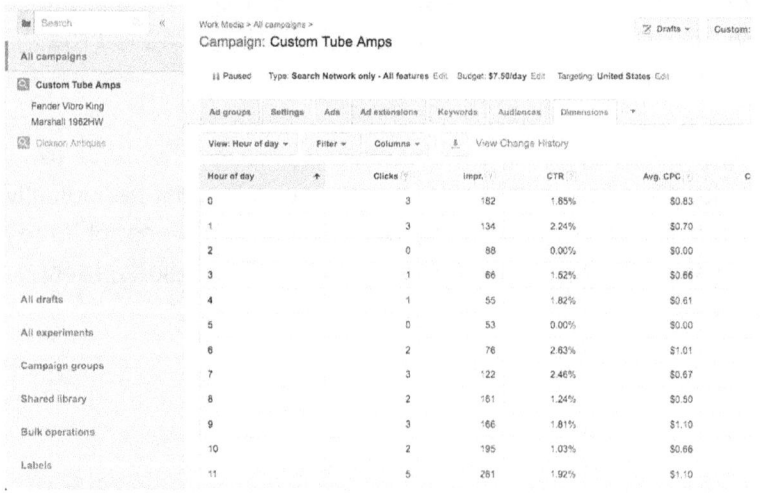

# AdSense (Content Network) Ads

There is another way you can use Google to advertise your business, which is by placing ads on websites that are part of the Google AdSense network. This is a little different because you are placing graphical ads on websites that are relevant to your target market, but not Google search results pages.

MOTORSPORTS
Ford GT Comes Second After 12 Hours at Sebring

MOTORSPORTS
Mustang GT4 Gets First Win in Sebring!

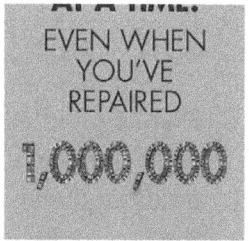

Google image ad on a Ford Mustang fan site.

VIDEOS
Wet Road + Mustang = Internet Infamy

For example, let's say you are a financial planner based in Bellevue. You could run graphical ads on websites related to financial topics, and target them to people within a certain geographic radius of Bellevue.

The websites where your ad appears will be private websites run by various people who have signed up for the AdSense program to make money on advertising. In our financial planner's case, his ads would run on websites related to finance.

You will find that the click-through-rates of content network ads are less than that from search engine results page ads, but you often also pay less for those clicks. Ultimately, the thing that matters most is your cost per conversion and return on investment. Where are you getting the most conversions at the best cost? It might be search ads or it could be content network ads.

You can run content network ads through the same campaigns you run search ads. But I would suggest you keep them separate and run content network ads in their own campaigns. When setting up a new campaign, you specify if you want to run ads in search, on content network sites, or both. Just pick one or the other.

## Dimensions

Pieces of data like the time of day and day of week are referred to as "dimensions" in Google AdWords. There are a bunch of different dimensions you can analyze. We have talked some about the time dimensions, although hour of day and day of week are not the only ones you can look at. You can break it down by month, hour, year, etc.

Some of the other things you can look at include geography, which breaks down all the way to the ZIP code level, the search terms used in your account (which are not the same as the keywords set up in your account), and the final destination URLs at which the visitors arrive.

Google wants to make money (and they are very good at it) but they also want you to be successful, so they provide you with all kinds of information you can use to improve your account performance. You're going to need to spend some time in your account to learn how to analyze this data and use it to make adjustments.

## Ad Extensions

Add extensions are very useful because they allow you to add additional information to your ad, or just make them bigger. I will briefly run through a couple of them.

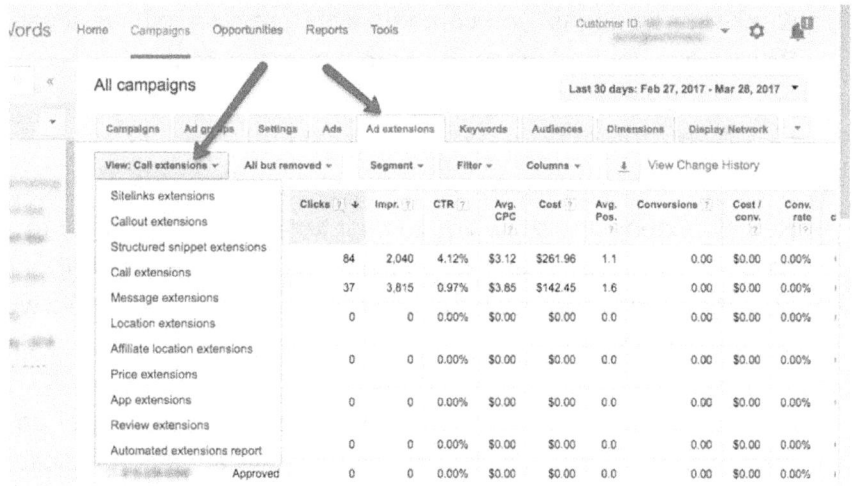

## Call Extension

Call extensions add your phone number to your ads. This is very good information to have in your ad because it makes you seem more legitimate and provides one additional way for customers to get in touch with you. It also adds the phone number to your ad without taking space away from copy.

## Site Links Extension

The site links extension allows you to add links to specific pages of your website to your ad. Google doesn't always show these, but sometimes it will. Our car dealer is a handy example in this case. Maybe he has a page on his website to go to Ford vehicles, a page devoted to cars, and a page devoted to Jeeps. Each of those separate pages would be a good candidate for a site link in the ad.

## Call Out Extension

Call out extensions allow you to add a call out such as "Call today for an appointment," "Make an appointment now," or "Big sale this weekend." I suggest you come up with a reason to have a call out. It will make your ad bigger and draw attention to it.

### Review Extension

Review extensions allow you to post text from a third-party review as part of your ad. However, this needs to be a review that is live on a third-party website that Google can verify. An example would be reviews on Yelp.

All of these add extensions make your ad physically bigger on the search results page, increasing their chance at getting noticed. They also provide more information to the user. I would suggest you spend some time on these things and figure out how to use the extensions that make sense for your ads.

## Remarketing

Remarketing is a very powerful concept. Have you ever noticed how if you visit a particular website or business, afterwards you will start seeing ads for that business following you around on other websites? That is remarketing.

Conversion rates and cost per conversion for remarketing ads can be outstanding. Remarketing only happens when people see your ad on content network websites. They are not search engine ads.

The specifics of setting up a remarketing campaign are beyond the scope of this book. If you have trouble figuring out how to do it based on Google's instructions, it is probably worth consulting an AdWords professional.

Here is the Google support page with instructions on how to set up remarketing:

https://support.google.com/adwords/answer/3210317?hl=en

Needless to say, remarketing is a powerful tool because it takes advantage of a basic marketing principle, which is that advertising is much more effective when exposed multiple times to its audience.

### Negative keywords

Negative keywords are keywords that should prevent an ad from being displayed. Let's say you sell lawn mowers, but you don't sell Husqvarna brand mowers. In this case, it might be useful to prevent your ad from appearing for visitors searching for Husqvarna mowers. So "Husqvarna" could be set up as negative keyword so that your ad does not display in those cases.

Negative keywords can be set up at the campaign level or as a shared library item, which allows you to use the same negative keywords across different campaigns. The key to making effective use of negative keywords is to keep an eye on the search terms that are bringing traffic to your website.

You should regularly monitor your search terms (from the Dimensions section of AdWords) to identify words that should be added as keywords, and those that should be added as negative keywords.

## Bing Ads

You can also try Bing Ads. Bing includes ads on both the Bing search engine as well as Yahoo. The two together account for about 10% of the search market, compared to about 80% for Google. However, 10% can still be a whole lot of people. Now, at the local level, it may not represent enough traffic to make any difference. But you really don't know until you try it. And if it works, you might find that your Bing traffic is more cost effective than your Google traffic.

To try Bing, go to https://advertise.bingads.microsoft.com.

Bing works pretty much the same way as Google AdWords, so I'm not going to go into any more detail about it here. Not all features will be the same, but the big stuff is. Your account will be divided out into campaigns and ad groups, with your ads and keywords being contained in the ad groups. If you are running AdWords ads, you can port your Google ads over to Bing to start with.

The trick is to make sure you measure performance, whether you're running Google ads, Bing ads, or anything else. If you don't have statistics for each different technique, then you won't really know what works and what doesn't.

## Split Testing

One of the biggest advantages of paid search marketing is that it allows you to perform split testing of ad copy and other marketing variables in a very cost-effective way. It is possible that one advertisement for your product or service could greatly outperform other ads. Testing different versions of your advertisement to see what works best is called split testing.

Split testing has been done for many years, but it has often been a very expensive procedure. With Google AdWords and other similar online advertising platforms, split testing is very simple because all you have to do is create multiple ads for your ad groups, and the advertising platform will automatically rotate the ads for you.

One thing to caution against: ultimately, conversion data is the most important thing you should use to judge your performance. Getting lots of clicks is great, but getting conversions is way better. For that reason, I suggest that you set your ad groups to rotate ads evenly.

Depending on your settings, Google will use click-through-rates to automatically spend more on ads that have a better click-through-rate. But it could very well be that another ad that has a lower click-through rate has a higher conversion rate, in which case Google would cause you to spend more on the lower performing ad.

In the end, you need to use your own eyeballs and brain to determine what is working and what is not, and make account changes accordingly. Avoid just automating everything so that Google makes all the decisions for you. I do believe that Google wants you to be successful...but Google is also very good at getting your money regardless of account performance.

## Paid Search Landing Pages

Most people link their paid search ads to one of the regular pages of their site. However, you might get better performance if the landing pages, or destination URLs, for your paid search ads are not the same as the regular pages of your website. You need to think about this strategically.

If a person clicks on your ad and arrives at your home page, he may not immediately find the information he is looking for. You need to send that visitor to exactly the page that has the information he wants.

You need to think like a direct marketer. Direct marketing usually involves presenting your prospective customer with a specific offer. It's not so much "Hey, my business is great," but more like "Hey, my business is great. Come see me now and save $50." The difference is that in direct marketing you are presenting a specific offer. Often multiple offers are split test to see what is most persuasive.

Remember that with paid search marketing, you are paying for every click to your website. Therefore, you may have better results by using some kind of specific offer. In fact, one good strategy is to only give the user a single option of what to do on a landing page. Typically this will be to contact you either via a form on the page or over the phone. But there will be no more options on the page. Not even a menu. All you want to do is have that person perform a single action.

This direct marketing style is not appropriate for every type of business. Take our car dealer. He probably does not want to limit the user to a single thing to do, instead of making it easy for the user to browse his entire inventory.

The conversion tracking script that you will use on your form confirmation page can be of a general nature - just to tell you that there was a visitor - or it can be revenue specific. In other words, if someone makes a purchase, the script can report that.

This is a step up in terms of technical difficulty because some programming has to take place in order for the website to pass the e-commerce information to the script. That's another one of those things that I'm not really going into details about here, but seek the help of a qualified website developer if you need someone to add this functionality to your website.

Another thing that you want to measure is performance from desktop computers versus mobile devices. Some businesses lend themselves very well to mobile devices. And it is certainly no secret that more and more search activity is taking place on mobile devices, often via voice search.

So if your data shows that you are performing better on mobile devices, or vice versa, you should adjust your bids appropriately to account for that. Google allows you to adjust your bids so that you spend more on the type of device that works best for you.

To adjust bids for different devices, click Settings, then Devices. Then click the little dash in the "Bid adj" column for the device you want to adjust, as shown below.

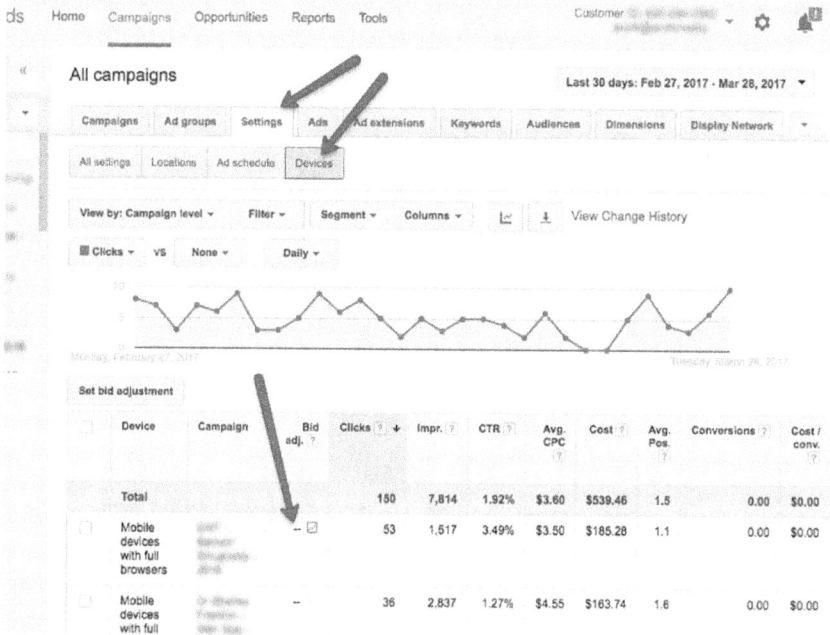

You are going to need to make sure that your website is mobile friendly. Really, your website needs to be mobile friendly anyway, but especially if you are spending money to drive traffic to it from mobile search.

# Social Media

Another big part of the Internet marketing equation is using social media, especially Google+ and Facebook. I don't really know anyone who uses Google+ for pleasure the way that people use Facebook. However, in terms of affecting search visibility in Google, Google+ is more important. This makes sense when you consider that Google+ is, obviously, owned by Google.

Facebook provides the best opportunity for a local business to push its marketing message in front of prospective customers in its local area. I have also found it to be a lower cost source of paid clicks than Google.

I don't do a whole lot with Twitter. I don't think it is as useful to local level businesses as Facebook and Google+, but it can certainly be effective if you have time for it. For our purposes here, I am going to focus mostly on Facebook and Google+ as I believe they are the social media sites most important for local level businesses.

To be successful with social media, you're going to have to take advantage of the concept of reciprocity. In other words, if you want people to like your page in Facebook, follow you on Twitter or Google+, or whatever, you are first going to have to do some liking and following yourself.

Many of the people and the Pages you like on Facebook or other social media platforms will like or follow you back in return out of politeness. I would say you could probably expect about one-fourth of them to do so.

Be proactive in liking and sharing content. This not only builds good will but it creates content for your own updates.

Let's consider an auto mechanic in a town called Fairview. After creating his Facebook page and beginning the process of posting his own content, he will want to begin following other people and businesses who are located in the Fairview area. If someone in the Fairview area who is on Facebook is looking for a good mechanic, you want him to know about you.

So as you follow people and businesses, you will begin to like their updates and share anything interesting on your own timeline. People on Facebook are dying to have their updates liked and shared. When you do this, you create a connection with that person.

You also want other people and businesses in your area sharing your content. This effect is magnified if it involves businesses that are complementary to yours. In our mechanic's case, that would be mostly auto-related businesses.

So as our auto mechanic interacts with people and businesses in the Fairview area, his Page like count will grow, and his message will be seen in front of more and more people.

This is a process that needs to be done on an ongoing basis. Once a week is not enough. Try to do some kind of update every day, even if it is just sharing someone else's update. Keep in mind that the focus of your updates should not be "sell, sell, sell" unless you have a way to make that really interesting.

Pre-scheduling your posts can make your life easier. This is a good way to make sure that your account stays updated. Memes (discussed below), cartoons, photos and other interesting visual items are good candidates for this type of pre-scheduling.

Humor works very well if you can figure out a way to work it into your updates. But by that I don't just mean re-posting funny material from other people, I mean having a humorous and self-deprecating attitude about yourself and your business. If something funny happens at your business, then post it as an update. In other words, make yourself likable. If you can make people laugh, that's even better.

Example: Sometimes I spend a day helping my wife around her antique store. The store has a nice little music section (that's my part of the store). One morning, just for fun, I decided to play on a drum kit that I had set up. The first time I struck the snare drum, water flew everywhere. Say what? Apparently we had had a roof leak, and my drums had gotten covered in water. So I decided to take advantage of it and make a short video of me playing the drums, with water flying everywhere, and post it as a store update. It was a pretty cool little video that did well in terms of likes.

I guess the point is to look for reasons to post anything funny or interesting, even if you have to make fun of yourself.

Got a roof leak? Make a video out of it.

Somebody passes out in front of your business (this happened at the antique store as well)? Make a video out of it.

Video is something that works well. And these days, at least for social media updates and such, you really don't need anything more than your phone. Now, if you make video a cornerstone of your marketing in general, then you will want to invest in some good quality video recording and audio equipment. However, for doing Facebook updates, all you have to do is prop your phone up, hit the record button, and start recording. I'm assuming you have a smart phone for video recording and upload. If not, get one. It's hard to do local online marketing these days without a smart phone.

I would keep videos short, maybe two or three minutes or less, unless you really have something fascinating to tell your viewers about. After you do the video, promote the post to an audience specifically tailored to the video. For instance, our car dealership might post a video about a new Ford Mustang they just got in. After posting the video, boosting it toward people who have shown interest in Ford or Mustangs would be a great idea.

Contests are also a great way to spread your message on Facebook. It used to be very restricted how you could do this, requiring some kind of paid Facebook app most of the time. Luckily, a while back Facebook relaxed the rules so that you can now simply ask people to like a post in order to enter a contest.

So now a contest is as simple as posting some kind of interesting content, and telling your Facebook friends that all they all they have to do is like the post to enter. I believe Facebook technically does not allow sharing of the content as a requirement, but you are certainly allowed to request that your friends share the post.

I usually state that you must both like and share an update to enter the contest. Then I request that you let me know you entered in the comments to the update. The problem is that you can't actually see everyone who shares your updates, so if you ask people to let you know they did it, at least you have that to go by.

Running a contest like this is not all that scientific. To pick a winner, take the list of people who liked the update (again, you won't really know who shared it and who didn't) and pick a winner at random.

Obviously, you need to have some kind of prize that is attractive enough to cause people to want to enter the contest. This could be something you sell, or it could just be something that people would want.

There are still third-party apps that can allow you to set up a more sophisticated contest, including automated random picking of a winner. You will probably need something like that if you want to do anything more advanced than what I discussed above. My point is that getting started with contests is as simple as asking people to like a post in order to enter.

One point to emphasize when promoting a local contest is that odds are good. If only 30 or 40 people enter the contest (which would not be unusual for a local business), then those who enter have much better odds than the typical contest.

Facebook events are another way to drive traffic to a business. In my antique store example, we will occasionally have an open house or special sale, which we can promote by setting it up as an event.

The last thing I'll say about your Facebook updates is that they should be interesting and visual. Don't just do text updates. As people are scrolling through their Facebook account, they may very likely pass over something that is straight text because it doesn't pop out at them. So it should contain an image or video, even if most of the content revolves around text.

Now, as for this whole knowing and liking thing, I am going to give you some seriously good advice right now. Honestly, I should redirect you to a link on my website where you are forced to pay $50 to download a PDF of instructions.

However, because I am feeling generous, I'm going to go ahead and give you this advice for free (the price of this book notwithstanding).

Here it is:

Be nice.

Be friendly.

Be honest.

Be helpful.

That's it. It's amazing how effective being nice is as a marketing strategy. People like to help people who they like. So if you are known as a friendly, nice person, people are more likely to help your business grow.

Not to go off on a diatribe, but it kills me how many businesses suffer from lack of friendly. I'll tell you what – being friendly can make or break you. There is an auto shop in Dickson, Tennessee, where I live, called Buster's Garage, and the owner of the shop (whose name, shockingly, is Buster) is one of the nicest men I have ever met.

One morning my truck broke down on the way to take my kids to school very near his garage. I had never met Buster before. But he drove my kids to school, drove me home (we talked about Vols football on the way), and after taking a look at my truck, said it was not the kind of thing he could fix, so I would have to take it to a specialist. He didn't charge me a nickel for any of it.

Do you think I remembered all that? I have returned to use his service several times since. And I'm writing about it now in my book. It's got nothing to do with Internet marketing, but everything to do with having a successful business.

## Google+

You will want to create a Google+ account for your business. To get started, go to [https://plus.google.com/](https://plus.google.com/).

I am assuming you have already created a Google business page for your business as explained earlier. If not, go do that first. Then come back and create a Google+ account.

Configure the account completely, using every option there is. Give it a background header. Upload as many photos as it will let you. Add as much information as you possibly can. When someone visits your Google+ page, it should look complete.

Begin immediately to post updates in your Google+ account. If you publish articles and blogs on your website, then every time you do an update, that should be used as an update for Google+.

Anytime you find an interesting article, something to link to, or something you can comment on that is related to your industry or might be interesting to your followers, use it as an update.

After you have something to see on your account, start following other users of Google+. Many of them will follow you back in return. You should look for other users who are in the position of possibly needing your services or who are possible referral sources.

You should also put a plus button on your website so that anyone who is logged into Google can plus your website. This is very important for helping drive up search engine rankings. Google plus ones are very valuable.

## Facebook

Next, you should create a Facebook Page for your business. If you don't already have a personal Facebook account, you should set that up first. Then you can use that account to create your business Page. In Facebook, business Pages do not have their own login. Your login will be your personal account, and then you will access your business through that.

To set up your business page, log into Facebook and then go to https://www.facebook.com/pages/create.

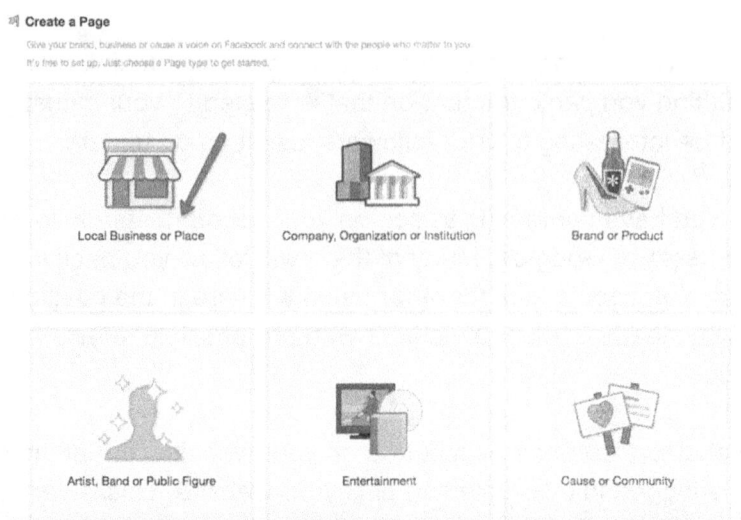

Facebook will have you select the type of business you have. For most of the business owners reading this, you will select the "Local Business" option. Then just follow the instructions.

Give your page an attractive header image and provide complete information about your business - location, hours of operation, etc. Add some photos, or videos if you have them. Even if you are just starting out, you need to have a Page that is attractive and interesting to visitors. Once the Page is set up, it is time to start doing updates.

Some of the keys to Facebook are:

- Post interesting content on a regular basis.

- Share content from other users.

- When you do an update that promotes your business, use Facebook's advertising system to boost it for more impressions. It is very difficult to build a Facebook following without boosting your posts. We will discuss this more later.

- Follow and like other people and business Pages that are in a position to refer you business or help you in any way. Do this as your business, and not as yourself.

Say a data networking company has a new kind of IP telephone system. It could do an update with photos of its employees installing the system in a well-known local business, along with some persuasive copy about how the system can save your business money or help you be more efficient.

The first thing you are going to want to do is go out and follow some businesses in your market area (either in terms of geographic proximity or who are in a related industry). The idea is to make connections with businesses who are possible referral sources or direct sources of business.

This is obvious if you are in a business-to-business situation. If you are selling stuff to other businesses, then make Facebook connections with other businesses who might have need for what it is you're selling, or whose customers could benefit from your services. But the concept also applies to businesses that sell to consumers.

It is important that you do things in Facebook as your business, and not just as you personally. This includes following other businesses and liking, commenting, or sharing their updates. It is not extremely obvious how to do this, and Facebook often changes how this process works.

To like another business Page as your business, click the three little dots beneath its header graphic and select to like as your page. If you manage multiple pages, like I do, then you will need to select the particular page you wish to like as.

If this has changed by the time you read this, don't blame me. Blame FaceBook and its management who can never make up their minds about how this stuff is supposed to work.

You need to view the Facebook feed of the business Pages that you follow as your business. To do that, at the time of this writing, go to your Facebook home page by clicking the Facebook logo. Then click the Pages Feed link on the left-hand menu. You may have to click the View More link to expand the menu to see it. You will then see the updates of all the pages you follow.

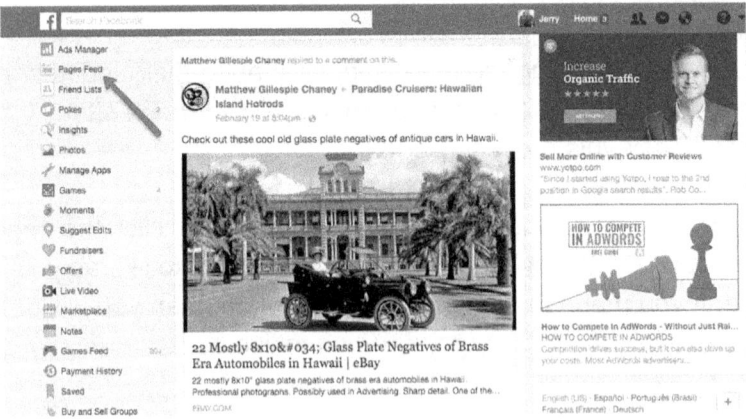

To like or comment on an update from another page, click the small arrow at the lower right-hand corner, and then select your business name. Then your like or comment will be recorded as coming from your business.

One point I would also like to make about Facebook is that you should not put all your marketing effort into promoting your Facebook page. You do not own your Facebook page – Facebook does. If Facebook goes away or decides you can't have a Page anymore, you're screwed. Ultimately, you want people coming to a property that you own. That would be your own website.

## Memes

You may not know what the word "meme" means. But you have definitely seen them. A meme is really any piece of media that gets passed around. Memes are those cute little graphics or funny pictures with humorous or philosophical sayings that people love to share on their social media accounts.

They can be a good way to feed your social media accounts with easy content that people might be prone to liking or sharing. You should not rely on them as your only source of content, but they are a good way to keep some kind of content flowing and to encourage others to share your stuff.

I am involved with a startup that sells a software type product to the construction industry (ProfitDig), and I have used memes as one source of content for its Facebook Page. In this case, what I did was go to Pinterest and search for funny construction related images or cartoons. Then I pre-scheduled a number of updates using those images.

There are also programs you can use that will create memes for you by combining an image of your choice with whatever words you want to use. An example of this would be the image of a famous person combined with a quote from that person.

One advantage to creating your own meme is that you can brand it with your own logo or other material. If people are going to pass something around via your social media accounts, you might as well get credit for it.

## Going viral

Sharing is the key to making social media work. You've probably heard the expression "going viral." This basically refers to the act of multiple people sharing some piece of information to their social media accounts, and then multiple other people sharing it from those accounts, and so on.

For example: If you post something on your Facebook Page, and five people share it to their own timelines, and then five people share it from each of those timelines....then your update appears on 25 timelines, exposing it to many hundreds or even thousands of people who would not have seen it otherwise.

If you have really fascinating content, then you might be able to pull this off simply by doing your updates. However, sometimes it is hard to get people to share your updates, even if they know who you are. So often what you have to do is basically bribe people to share your stuff.

Here's an example.

In our antiques business, we update Facebook regularly with really nice photos of interesting items in the store. People will sometimes share them either on their own timeline or with other people they know who they think will be interested in those items.

But shares exploded when we started doing some simple Facebook contests whereby visitors could enter to win an interesting prize by liking and sharing an update. The update would be about the prize you could win. Liking and sharing is such an easy way to enter a contest that many people were doing it just because they had a chance to win something without doing a lot of work. And their odds were good.

I have used this same concept with ProfitDig, where you could win a free copy of a book we wrote and a cap or shirt. Bribery works.

## Facebook Advertising

Facebook advertising can be very effective and much less costly than using something like Google AdWords. However, unlike Google, who are masters at reaching into your pocket to get your money, Facebook tends to make things way harder than they need to be.

The easiest way to start advertising on Facebook is by boosting your posts. What this means is that you pay money to have your update appear to other Facebook users, whether they follow your Page or not.

When you boost the post, you should select an audience that is targeted toward the subject of the post. Let's say our auto dealer posts an update about a new Ford pick up truck. "Ford" would be a great interest to use for targeting. In other words, you're telling Facebook that you would like to show your update featuring a Ford pickup truck to people who have shown an interest in Ford vehicles.

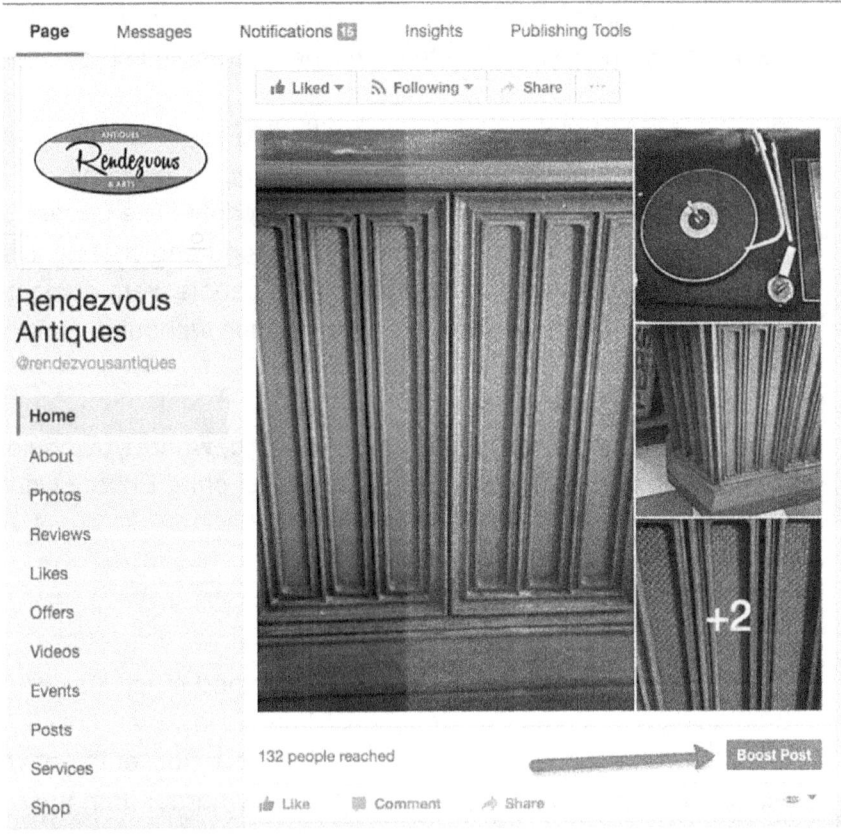

You can also target by sex and age, which is often a good idea. For instance, an antique store that does an update about doilies would probably be better off targeting women, and maybe women of a particular age range. Men who work in garages probably aren't all that interested in doilies.

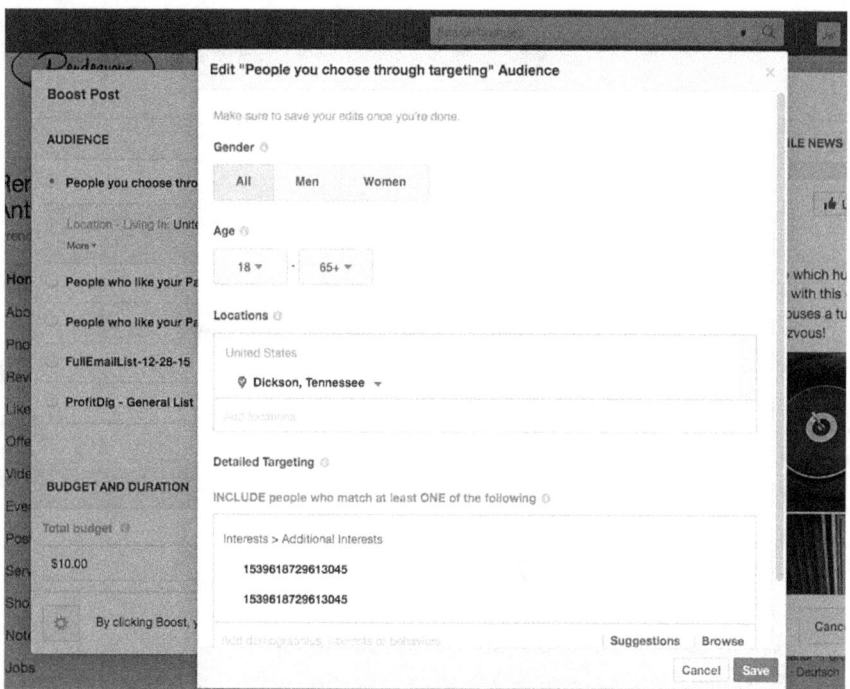

If you are just trying to get your message in front of everyone in a particular geographic area, you can just target that area. If you take that approach, you should have a very limited geographic area in mind unless you have a huge budget. Try boosting your post for $10 to everyone in New York City, and you will be out of budget in about a second. Your message would be like a spec of sand in a dessert. But do the same thing in Centerville, Tennessee, and your post might run all day.

Facebook will show you how many impressions, clicks and such you got from paid boosted impressions versus organic impressions. Especially early on, you will probably find that you get many, many more impressions from your boosted updates.

Boosting your posts is not the only way to advertise on Facebook. Another option is to just create a standalone ad promoting your Page or business. To do that, go to your Ads Manager page (which you can access from the main menu on the left-hand side of the screen of the main Facebook page), and then click the Create Ad button.

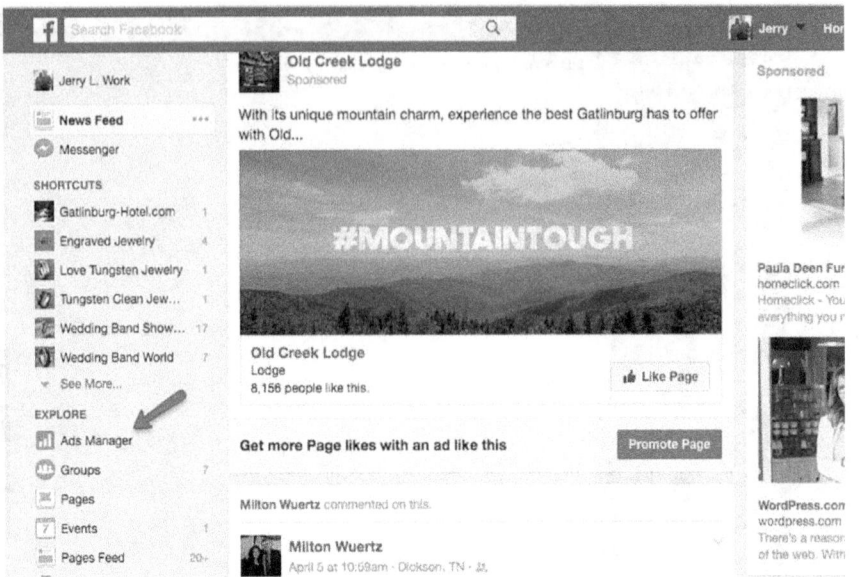

At this point, the process becomes similar to running ads on Google. You will name your campaign, set your targeting, set your daily budget, write the ad copy, etc. One thing about Facebook that I have never liked is that it is not as transparent as Google with regards to how much you should expect to pay per click. I will say, however, it will likely be less per click (or engagement) than you would pay in Google.

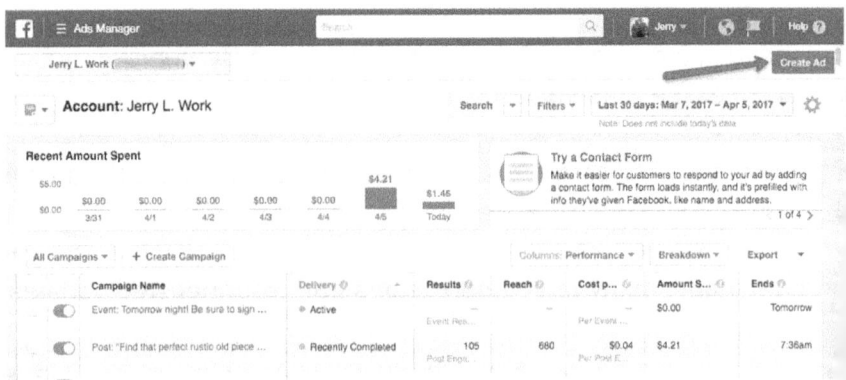

Likes on your Facebook page are certainly not the same thing as someone actually giving you money. But what you're doing is building name recognition among your target market, presenting them a marketing message, and helping improve your search engine rankings. All of this stuff just serves to put people in the pipeline (your sales funnel). Then you still have to persuade those people to be your customer.

None of this will help you generate sales if you do not have a good product or service and provide good customer service. It also helps to be likable, as I discussed earlier.

Videos are great content for Facebook updates as well. If you can show some real personality or make them very funny, people might share them. But I would also boost them as well.

Try to get 1,000 likes for your Page. Then keep going. You won't get to a thousand without working your account.

At our antique store, we only did about four or five updates a week. But we put effort into making the updates interesting, and we would usually spend $5 or $10 to boost them. So I would advise you to do something similar. Post interesting updates and spend $10 or less to boost them. If you are strategic in your targeting, then in less than a year you will have 1,000 Page likes, which is a good base.

Facebook recently released something called Business Manager, which is a way to manage multiple Facebook advertising accounts from a single login. Great idea, but it's not the easiest thing to use. My advice is to avoid Business Manager unless you manage multiple Pages for other people. Otherwise, you will just be making things complicated for yourself. But again, by the time you read this, Facebook will probably have changed the whole way thing works anyway. So in that case...never mind.

Most of my social media discussion here has focused on Facebook because it is the platform that I think is most important for local small businesses. It still allows you the highest degree of interaction with potential clients and is the one most likely used by your potential customers.

## YouTube and Videos

Videos should be used for social media updates, as discussed earlier, as well as added to your YouTube channel.

To set up a YouTube channel, first log into your Google account, then go to https://www.youtube.com and click the Sign in button. Then just follow the instructions. What you are going to do is set up your own "channel" - which is like your own little Internet TV channel.

Optimize your videos for specific keywords. Use the keywords in your video titles and descriptions. When uploading a video to YouTube, look at the description more like a complete webpage than just a brief description. Google loves video. There have been times in my work when I was able to get a YouTube video ranked very highly for high competition keywords.

YouTube also has its own video advertising system that can work very well for generating views of your videos to target audiences at a very low cost.

After posting a video to YouTube, use it for social media updates, website updates, etc.

# Email

By now, email may seem like sort of an old fashion way of doing things. But the fact is it still works if you do it correctly. What you want to do is build your own email list of people who know who you are, who voluntarily agreed to receive your messages, and who are in a position to purchase or refer your products or services.

Having your own list of people who have volunteered to receive messages from you is a powerful position to be in from a marketing standpoint. It is traditional marketing wisdom that it is much cheaper and easier to sell to people who have already bought from you in the past. Retail businesses can do something as simple as have a notebook next to their register to encourage visitors to sign up for their list. As long as you actually take the time to transfer those email addresses to your server, this is a very effective way to build a list of local customers.

Regardless if you have a brick and mortar location or not, It is a fantastic idea to have an email signup form on your website. Make it prominent. If someone really likes your business or your website and is willing to voluntarily receive email messages from you, then you should make it REALLY easy to do so. That signup form will also serve as the conversion event you use to measure performance from other marketing channels such as paid search.

One thing to keep in mind is that people have short memories. Once they sign up, you should begin to send emails quickly and regularly. Some of this can be automated. You can use a tool called an autoresponder to send a pre-programmed series of email messages to new subscribers.

The reason it is so important to capture email addresses if possible is that once a visitor to your website has left, if you haven't created some way to get back in touch with them (in this case, their email address) then you have lost that visitor. He has come and gone and now you have no way to sell to him.

As you build up your email list, you are going to need it to send out emails on a regular basis, and it can't all be automated. It is a good idea to send email newsletters that are not just promotional in nature but that also provide useful information to the reader. People are much less likely to unsubscribe from your list if you provide them value.

## Email Marketing Companies

You will need to sign up with an email list company. Here are a few that are popular:

- www.constantcontact.com
- www.mailchimp.com
- www.sendgrid.com
- www.verticalresponse.com
- www.myemma.com

There are probably many more, but the above listed companies are all very reputable and have been in business a long time. I honestly can't recommend any one. I am currently using mostly Mailchimp. But any of the above companies will work just fine.

## Email Signup Form

Your email list company will provide you with the code you need to use on your website to allow visitors to sign up. What will happen is that when the signup form is submitted, the information will be submitted to the email server to add to your list. What you want to happen after that is for the email company server to redirect the visitor to a thank you / confirmation page.

That thank you page is where your paid search conversion script will reside, if you are running ads. So if you are using paid search, every time a paid visitor arrives at your website and signs up for your list, you know what ad and keyword resulted in the conversion.

In Google Analytics, you would set the thank you page as a goal. Every time someone submitted the form and arrived at that page, it would be reported in analytics as a conversion. This will tell you how many conversions happened from organic search, paid search, social media, email, or anything else.

One thing Google Analytics won't show you is exactly what organic Google search queries were used. It's a whole security-related thing I won't go into. But you can pretty much find out everything else from Google Analytics.

As far as the design and layout of the email you send out, your email list provider will likely have templates you can use that will give the email a very professional look. Just select a template, add your content and images, and the email should look very professional.

I also highly advise that you send a test email to yourself first to make sure that everything looks correct.

You can add emails to your list outside of your website. For example, many local retail shops will have a book sitting on the counter in which store customers or visitors can add their email address. The shop owner can then manually add these emails to his list.

It is perfectly acceptable for you to add anyone with whom you have done business to an email list even if they have not specifically done so themselves or requested that you do it.

Here is one more thing to know about email. It is NOT illegal for you to add anyone you want to an email list. As long as you abide by one's wish to be removed from your list, then you can send an email to anyone you want.

# Analytics

Analytics is performance information about your website. It means things like:

- How many people have visited your website.
- Where those people came from.
- How long they stayed on your website.
- What pages they visited.

I shouldn't have to tell you, but I will anyway: it is very important to know how your website is performing. Analytics will also help you figure out your return on investment - how many dollars you are making for every dollar you spend on your marketing.

There are different options for analytics, but these days most businesses use Google Analytics. Here is what to do:

- Visit www.google.com/analytics and follow the instructions to log in or create a Google account if you don't have one.

- Once you are signed into a Google Analytics account, get the Google analytics script by clicking the admin icon (that looks like a gear) on the main menu.

- Look for the link that says "Tracking Info." Click that, then click the link that says "Tracking Code."

- Copy and paste the code that it presents to you on every page of your website.

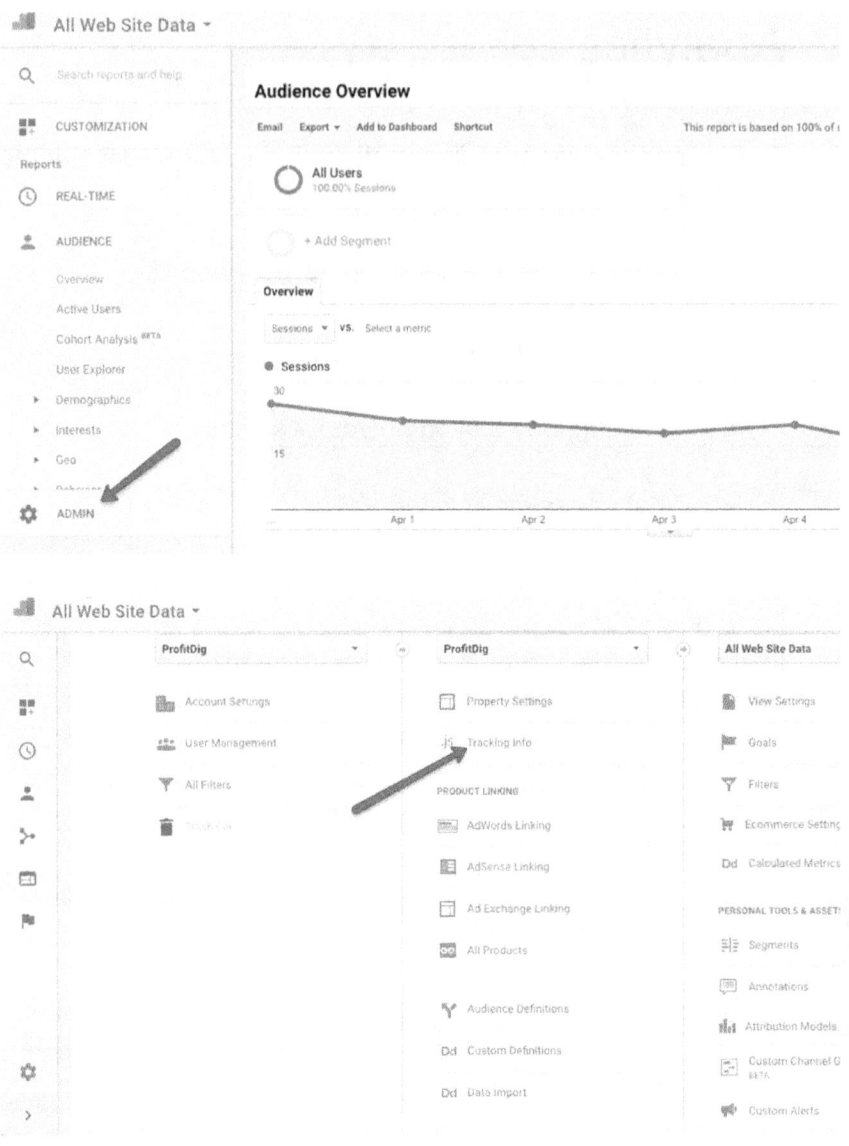

That is a super quick description of how this process works as of this writing, but Google changes this stuff up all the time. The main point is to find the Google analytics code, wherever it is, and paste it into every page of your site. Most likely, you will only have to paste it into a single footer file, which will update all of the pages automatically.

Analytics can be a complicated topic, so I'm not going to take up a whole lot of time talking about it here. But don't skip this step. Getting analytics installed on your website is the first and most important step in gauging the performance of your Internet marketing.

## Conversion Tracking

In marketing, it is very important to remember that the whole point of all of it is to generate conversions. A conversion is the accomplishment of a specific goal. In its most basic form, a conversion is when someone gives you money. If you sell a product directly from your website, then tracking conversions is easy.

But very often, especially at the local level, marketing is used to generate leads but not necessarily direct online sales. In that case, you have to be a little more creative in figuring out how to count conversions. One way is to set up "goals" in your analytics account. A goal is something in particular that happens on your website that you would consider the completion of a conversion. Most of the time, this will be the loading of a particular web page.

Maybe your conversion goal for a particular marketing campaign is to get people to sign up for your mailing list. In that case, a conversion would happen when someone signs up for your mailing list. After someone submits the form to sign up for your mailing list, he is redirected to a "thank you" page.

That thank you page should only load in someone's browser after submitting the form. So if submission of the signup form is considered a conversion, then you would set the URL of the thank you page as a goal. Once you do this, analytics will tell you all kinds of things about the people who sign up for your list.

If you use Google AdWords or another advertising platform, you will likely have a separate conversion tracking script to use.

Google has a service called Tag Manager that can make it easier to manage multiple tracking scripts. To learn more about that, visit www.google.com/analytics/tag-manager.

**Conversion Rate**

Conversion rate is the percentage of people who have been exposed to your marketing who convert.

So if you run an ad on Google, and it gets 500 clicks, and 5 of those visitors convert, then your conversion rate is 1% (5 / 500).

In Internet marketing, cost per acquisition, as discussed above, is usually called cost per conversion.

# Other Internet Marketing Strategies

Here are some strategies that are sort-of outside the categories we discussed above.

## Increasing Search Shelf Space

One thing you need to keep in mind is that if you are operating in a limited geographic market, there is probably going to be a limited amount of search engine traffic related to your product or service. So you need to be aggressive in finding ways to get as much of that search engine traffic as you can.

All of the website listings that appear on a page in Google for a search can collectively be called "shelf space." You want as much of that shelf space as you can get.

One way to increase your shelf space is to use both paid search as well as SEO for organic listings. If a search results page has one organic listing for your business and one paid listing, then you have doubled your search visibility.

Another way to increase your visibility for particular search is to have pages outside of your main site rank. Expired domains, which we will discuss shortly, are useful for this. The idea is to build web pages optimized for your target keywords so that they rank along with your main site.

Similarly, you can build a pages on third party platforms like WordPress.com and Blogger.com that have a good chance of ranking.

If you use this strategy of building out optimized pages on various platforms outside your website, you don't really want Google to make the connection between all of the other pages and your business. For that reason, it is a good idea to link out to lots of other web pages and not just your own website.

## Craig's List

One area of Internet marketing that some small businesses rely upon too much, and others not at all, is the use of online classified ad sites such as Craig's List.

You want people to find your business online one way or another - period. The fact is Craig's List has tens of millions of users who really do use it to search for products or services.

Here is a quick primer on using Craig's List.

Visit the website www.craigslist.com. Make sure that you are in the appropriate city. The Craig's List site will automatically load the city that it thinks is most appropriate for you. For example, when I visit www.craigslist.com, it automatically redirects to nashville.craigslist.com, because Nashville is the nearest city. If Craig's List does not redirect you to the appropriate city, you can find it by clicking on your state on the right-hand side of the page, and then selecting the best city.

Then click the "post to classifieds" link in the upper left corner. Select a category for your post. Then create your post, which will include a title and description. It may also include a price if that is appropriate.

Make sure the title speaks clearly and specifically to the product or service being offered. There could even be an SEO advantage if you can work a keyword or two in smoothly.

In the description, at the top use a few adjectives to describe the service:

Reliable paint repair

Experienced, trustworthy accounting
Affordable carpet cleaning
Safe and secure storage

You get the idea.

List all of the things you can do, at least relevant to the category for the ad, and talk about why someone should hire you. How many years of experience do you have? How many companies have you done work for? What accommodations have you received?

Post photos in the ad, and make them of a high quality.

Finally, make it very clear how someone goes about getting in touch with you. If you want to be a real advertising guru, you should also include a full-blown call to action.

We only have five of these in stock so you better hurry.
Call us today to get started solving your problem.
Stop being a loser. Call us today and become a winner.

Etc.

I don't think you should depend on Craig's List as you're only means of generating business. It does not allow you to showcase yourself like your own website or social media. But it can be an effective piece of an Internet marketing campaign.

## Expired Domain Names

Domain names are the friendly website addresses that people use to load websites. An expired domain name is a website domain name that someone had registered at some point, but then for whatever reason allowed to expire. What that means is that you can then register that domain name for your own use.

It could be that you want to use the expired domain name for your own website, or it could be that you want to use the expired domain for search engine optimization purposes.

The reason an expired domain name can be valuable is because the previous owner may have gone through the process of generating links or doing other things to promote the site, which will help the site rank in Google or other search engines.

Another reason they are valuable is just because of their age. All else equal, the older the domain name, the better. So if you have the option of registering a brand new domain or an older one, you are better off going with the older domain. Because then you benefit from it being aged, as well as any link building that the previous owners may have done for the domain.

One convenient way to search for expired domain names is to visit the website www.expireddomains.net. This will allow you to search for expired domains using keywords. If you find a keyword domain that would work well for your business, you can register it either to have as your main business web address, or just for SEO purposes.

## Content Aggregation

You don't have to always come up with content on your own. You can borrow snippets of content from other websites and use that as the basis of your own content. For instance, you could post a paragraph from an article you find interesting, and then follow that up with a paragraph of your own commentary on the subject. As long as you give credit and a link to the original source, then that is fine.

In fact, using this strategy, you can actually help your website rank better. There is a word for this type of process, which is "content curation." And Google loves it.

Google loves the idea of information on a particular type of subject flowing from one website to another. This also relates to the trust flow concept that we discussed earlier. If Google comes to trust that your website is a good source of information on a particular subject and tends to link out to other good source of information on that subject, then it will be much more likely to give your website good search visibility.

Now more than ever, it is important not only to have links pointing to your website, but links pointing out as well. However, avoid the old trick of link swapping. Google is much less likely to place weight on the content and links of your website if links out are always returned.

That's not to say that local businesses shouldn't link to one another and that type of thing. What I am mostly talking about is having a regular system in place to swap links with other websites. Definitely avoid having pages on your website there are nothing but links you have swapped with other websites.

# Conclusion

Look y'all, I left out a mountain of details here. This book could easily be 5X longer if I REALLY went into specifics. But this is meant to be a somewhat high level overview of the things you need to do to promote your local business online, with enough detail to get you going.

Is this stuff easy? Not really. But it ain't rocket science either. The main thing is giving yourself the time to do it. If you can't find the time, then hire someone to do it for you. If you do seek outside help, the knowledge in this book will make sure that you understand what your Internet marketing guy is doing. You will be much less likely to be fooled.

I do invite you to contact my company, Work Media, if you don't know where to turn. We work with local businesses every day and we would be proud to work with you. You can call us at 615-375-8793, email us at info@workmedia.net, or visit us online at www.workmedia.net.

Good luck!

www.ingramcontent.com/pod-product-compliance
Lightning Source LLC
Chambersburg PA
CBHW061441180526
45170CB00004B/1514